WORDS CAN WORK™

When
Talking
With Kids
About

Sexual Health

By Jeanne Blake

BLAKEWORKS™

Published by Blake Works, Inc.
P.O. Box 1402 Gloucester, Massachusetts 01930, U.S.A.

First printing, May 2004

Copyright © Blake Works, Inc. 2004

Blake Works, Inc. is an authorized licensee of
the trademark Words Can Work™ owned by Jeanne Blake.

ISBN 0-9753147-0-X

Printed in the United States of America

Designed by Hird Graphic Design

Cover by Harbour Light Productions, Inc.

Portions of interviews have been reprinted with
the permission of Family Health Productions, Inc.

Note: Some names in this book have been changed to protect identities.

The content of this book is for informational purposes only.
It is not intended to replace professional advice. For specific advice
on talking with children or addressing specific issues,
please consult a medical or health professional.

Dedicated to my mother and father
for their love and willingness to listen.

Contributors

David Satcher, M.D., Ph.D.
Former U.S. Surgeon General
Director, National Center for Primary Care
Morehouse School of Medicine

Paula K. Rauch, M.D.
Chief, Child Psychiatry Consultation Service
Director, Cancer Center Parenting Program
Massachusetts General Hospital

Robert Hatcher, M.D., M.P.H.
Professor of Gynecology and Obstetrics
Emory University School of Medicine
Senior author, *Managing Contraception*
Senior author, *Contraceptive Technology*

Penny J. Hitchcock, D.V.M., M.S.
Former Chief, Sexually Transmitted Diseases Program
National Institute of Allergy and Infectious Diseases
Director, Prevention of AIDS and STDs in Adolescents

Contents

Words Can Work
When Talking With Kids About Sexual Health

Children are inundated by sexual messages from TV, radio, and the Internet. As a parent, you can balance these influences by talking openly with your child.

This can be challenging. Many parents grew up in homes where sex was rarely discussed. They aren't sure how or when to begin to talk about sex. Some worry they'll encourage the very behaviors they hope to prevent. Others believe they can delay these discussions until their child is a teen.

There is a more effective approach. Day to day, you can watch for opportunities to share your thoughts, to ask questions, and to listen to your children.

This book tells how some families talk about sexual health. Dr. David Satcher and Dr. Paula Rauch review each true story and offer the information — and the words — you can use to handle similar situations. Questions for self-reflection or group discussion follow each story. *Words Can Work: When Talking With Kids About Sexual Health* will help your family begin and continue important conversations. This is how you can raise sexually healthy children — kids who love and trust themselves and who make good choices.

Girls and puberty

FACT: The normal range of onset of puberty is age 8 to 14 in females.[1]

As children go through puberty, they need a lot of support. They experience dramatic physical and emotional changes. If you're a parent of a preadolescent or adolescent child, you know that his or her emotions can fluctuate by the minute. Surging hormones, in part, cause these changes and can affect how children feel about themselves and others.

By talking with their parents, other trusted adults, and well-informed older siblings, young people can share their concerns and get accurate information. They can learn that the changes they experience are a natural part of growing up.

Most children are curious about when they will reach puberty.[2]

Kate tries to attend all her 11-year-old daughter's soccer games. She wants to support her daughter, and she also enjoys the time with the other parents. They relax as they talk about family and work.

Kate remembers the time their conversation turned to puberty when one mom described the moods of her teenage child. "One minute we have smiles," she said, "and tears the next."

The experience was familiar. Kate said, "Sounds like hormones to me."

Kate shared a strategy she'd used when her daughter Maddy went through puberty and her moods changed. "Maddy asked why she'd cry, sometimes for no reason," Kate recalled. "I told her, 'You have hormones, honey. Chemicals that affect your moods.' "

Kate urged Maddy to chart her moods on the calendar. Doing that would help her anticipate irritable or sad feelings, she explained. It worked. Kate said it helped her, too, knowing when to give Maddy a little extra room.

Everyone liked Kate's idea. They wondered if she'd talk with *their* daughters. One mom offered to serve coffee to the mothers while Kate met privately with the girls. Kate agreed, under two conditions: the girls would choose the topics and whether they wanted to participate.

On the day of the gathering, 20 excited girls arrived ready to talk about menstruation. Kate displayed several sexual health books. "Take a little time to look at them," she said. "Let me know if you have questions. Everything we talk about stays between us."

The girls peppered Kate with questions: "When will my period start?" "Will blood gush out?" "What if I'm at my desk at school?" "What if

> *"Maddy asked why she'd cry, sometimes for no reason. I told her: 'You have hormones, honey.'"*
>
> Kate

I'm on the bus?" "Do tampons hurt?" "What if the blood comes through my clothes?" Kate answered one question after another. "When I didn't know the answer," Kate said, "we looked it up."

Asha, a petite girl, slowly asked, "Kate, when will I...?" She looked down at her undeveloped chest.

"When will you what?" Kate asked.

"When will I know this is what I'm stuck with?" Asha asked.

The other girls seemed relieved that someone had finally asked. "Yeah," they chimed in. "When *are* we going to get breasts?"

"Wow," Kate thought. "This is really the question of the day."

Kate explained that girls develop at different ages — some at 8 or 9 years old, others much later. Kate said she didn't get breasts until she was 14 years old, and it had earned her the nickname "Flatsie."

"Twenty sets of eyes fixed on my chest," she says. "I told them, 'Look at what I have now.' "

"So there's hope for me," Asha said with relief.

Kate asked the girls why breast size mattered so much. They answered that boys like girls with bigger breasts.

Many girls worry a lot about their first period — that they'll be unprepared and, as a result, feel humiliated and ashamed.[3]

"O.K., you guys, let's talk about this," Kate said. "Why do you like Tamara?"

The girls answered: "She's good at soccer." "She has a positive attitude." "She's funny."

"O.K.," Kate continued. "Why do you like Maddy?"

"She's strong," they said. "She's smart." They went around the room and pointed out each girl's best qualities.

"Denise," Kate said, "do you like Ashley because she has big breasts?"

"No!" Denise shrieked.

"Well, do you all like Corinne because she's getting breasts?"

"No!" everyone shouted.

Then why would they be interested in a boy who liked them only for their breast size? "Wouldn't you want a guy to like you because you're smart, easy to talk to, and funny? All the things you said?" Kate asked.

She continued, "If Vic married me only because of my looks, what would happen if I gained weight or had a breast removed? We married each other because of who we are, not how we look."

By the looks on their faces, Kate knew that the girls understood. "I'd never thought of

"Wouldn't you want a guy to like you because you're smart, easy to talk to, and funny?"

Kate

that," one girl commented. "It makes a lot of sense."

Kate told the girls they could get together again. If they had questions, they could ask her during car-pooling or, with their parents' permission, they could send her e-mails. Still, she encouraged them to ask questions in front of their friends. "That way," she said, "everyone can learn. And it's important to support each other."

Kate says that talking with the girls that afternoon was "the most beautiful moment educating, ever."

Consider This

Dr. Rauch: The frank tone Kate set helped the girls feel comfortable enough to ask a range of very specific questions about their worries on topics from menstruation to their appearance.

Dr. Satcher: In our society, girls too often get the message that they're valued only for their physical appearance. By creating an environment where the girls could talk freely, Kate helped the girls see that character is more important than the way someone looks.

Dr. Rauch: Kate was right to let the girls set the agenda and choose whether to attend. It was important that every girl in the room knew that her friends were eager to be there,

Dr. Satcher

"...Kate helped the girls see that character is more important than the way someone looks."

Dr. Satcher

"...our schools, communities of faith, businesses, and youth-serving organizations can create opportunities for young people to talk openly about sexual health."

and that what they talked about stayed between them. That helped them feel comfortable. The best conversations grow out of situations where young people are relaxed and don't feel forced to participate.

Dr. Satcher: Some children come from homes where the parents are well prepared to talk about these issues. Others do not. To ensure that children get the information they need, it's important to know when to ask for outside help.

Dr. Rauch: Asking for help when you need it, from other parents or from a professional, is part of being a good parent. Some of the moms may have hesitated to talk with their girls because they were afraid they'd be asked questions they couldn't answer. But many of the questions were easy. When Kate didn't know the answer, they turned to the books. If the other moms had heard how the conversation unfolded in a supportive environment, they may have been more willing to initiate conversations with their children.

Dr. Satcher: Kate offers a good example of how our schools, communities of faith, businesses, and youth-serving organizations can create opportunities for young people to talk openly about sexual health. Every child deserves this opportunity. It's as important as learning about one's mental and physical health. This process must always be respectful of a diversity of opinions and values.

Dr. Rauch: When these opportunities arise, parents need to know what's being taught, and to feel confident in the adults leading the discussion. Parents need to follow up with their child to discuss what they learned and how it fits with their family's values. A parent could ask, "What was most interesting to you?" "Did anything surprise you?" "Do you have questions for me?" These questions can serve as icebreakers for conversations at home.

Dr. Rauch

Ask Yourself

- How do I remind my child that her character matters more than her physical appearance?

- What opportunities do I create for my child to ask questions about her development?

- Do I hesitate to bring up certain topics with my child because I think I don't have enough information?

- Do I take time to learn the information I need to talk with my child about her development?

"Parents need to follow up with their child to discuss what they learned and how it fits with their family's values."

- When my child learns something new about her development, am I prepared to follow up and find out whether she clearly understands what she's learned?

- When I follow up, do I ask questions that can help my child think through important issues?

- Who could I turn to for help to teach my child about sexual health?

Remember

It's wise to ask for outside help to talk with your child when you need it, as Kate's friends did. But it's your right — and your responsibility — to share your own values about sexual health with your child. Take time to get the information you need to be a reliable source. It's important that concerns about saying everything perfectly don't interfere with your willingness to start and continue conversations with your child.

Kemba's story

Puberty began later for me than it did for my two best friends. That's when I started to look at guys with them. We'd be going down the street and say, "Wow, he's so fine. He's so cute." It was so much fun. I started to care more about what I looked like, too.

It's good when your body starts changing, because you're going into a new phase of your life. You're not a little girl anymore. You're going into pre-womanhood. You start to look at yourself in a different way.

Puberty can be a scary time if you don't have anyone to talk to about it. My mother died from breast cancer just as I was becoming a teenager. People like my Aunt Gloria recognized that I needed someone to talk to. She offered to explain things to me, like how my body was changing. She let me know that, if I needed to talk or had questions, she was always there.

"Puberty can be a scary time, if you don't have anyone to talk to about it."

Kemba

My dad was there for me a lot, too. One day he said, "Oh, by the way, we can go bra shopping." He dropped me off at the store and pretended he needed something down the street.

Ten minutes later he came back and asked if everything went O.K.

When I started to get my period, my dad was going to the store and asked me if I needed pads. By talking with me like that, my dad showed me it was O.K. to talk without embarrassment. We can still talk about anything. He's a great role model for me.

"...my dad showed me it was O.K. to talk without embarrassment."

Kemba

In puberty a lot of kids feel embarrassed about their body changing. If parents are comfortable talking, they give children an example to follow. If you have sisters, brothers, or friends who are older, they can help you through it, too, and explain what's happening.

Boys and puberty

FACT: The normal range of onset of puberty in males is age 9 to 15.[4]

Look into any middle or high school class and you'll see that boys and girls develop at different rates. Boys with an athletic build and boys who are the first to grow facial hair are often respected and looked up to by their peers. Boys who are slower to develop may wonder if they'll ever catch up with bigger guys, or whether they're normal.

Parents can't control the rate at which their children develop. But if they listen, get informed, and are available, they can help guide their children through these awkward times.

Mike was the last boy in his class to go through puberty. Now, as the father of two boys, he remembers how he struggled.

By the time he was 15 years old, Mike was 5 feet 2 inches tall. He was terrified that he'd stopped growing, and that his body would be hairless forever. "I remember crying and asking my mom, 'When will I grow?' "

His mother tried to reassure him. "Everything will work out for the best. Don't worry."

Mike's dad had a tough-guy attitude. "Rub a little dirt on it and get back into the game," was his approach.

But telling a 15-year-old boy not to worry didn't prepare Mike for a humiliating locker room experience.

"The athletes I hung around were my frame of reference," Mike says. "One day after football practice, I was in the shower. A big, hairy lineman walked in. He took one look at me and burst out laughing." He was Mike's friend but had never seen a hairless 15-year-old and thought he looked funny.

Forty years later, Mike recalls how inferior and helpless he felt. "It was one of the most significant events of my life," he says.

The football coach noticed that Mike was hurting. "He pulled me aside," Mike says. "He told me it was O.K. to be small. He reminded me that my dad, a successful businessman, was short. My coach was short too, and he did O.K." Mike's coach couldn't make him taller, but having his feelings acknowledged made Mike feel better.

Mike grew almost seven inches the next year. Looking back, he wishes his parents had explained that people grow and mature at different rates — some early, some late. "I hope parents talk with their kids and explain that how fast we grow depends partly on our genes," he says. "I watched my boys carefully. As it turned out, they developed along with their friends. If they hadn't, you can bet I'd have talked with them. I didn't want anything to undermine my children's sense of security."

Consider This

Dr. Satcher: When parents aren't responsive, as in Mike's case, children can feel isolated.

Dr. Rauch: Adolescence is a time of enormous self-consciousness. In any eighth- or ninth-grade class, you're likely to see guys who could appear to be 10 years old and guys who could pass for 18.

Dr. Satcher: When children are slower to develop, it can be very stressful for them. It's important they know that developing more slowly or more quickly doesn't mean there's something wrong with them.

Dr. Rauch: Not all children will bring their concerns to you. You have to be on the lookout.

Dr. Satcher: Right. Look for teachable moments. That's the key.

Dr. Rauch: Mike's sons developed along with their peers. Still, they might have benefited from hearing what their dad struggled with as a boy. He could have said, "When I was your

Dr. Rauch

"Not all children will bring their concerns to you. You have to be on the lookout."

age, I didn't have much hair on my body, and I was self-conscious about looking so much younger than my friends. But eventually I grew hair, too. Is there anything you feel self-conscious about?"

Ask Yourself

Reach out to children in your life so that they know you're available to support them as they grow up.

- How did I learn about sexual health as a child?

- How do I want my child to learn differently?

- What aspects of my own upbringing would I like to repeat with my child?

- Do I watch for signs — such as a reluctance to go to gym class or to parties — that indicate my child may feel self-conscious about his development?

- What experiences from my own childhood can I share with my child to help him understand that what he's experiencing is normal?

Remember

Consider how you can reach out to your children so that they know you're available to support them. You can ask: "Do kids tease each other in the locker room?" "How do you feel about the way you look tonight?" These questions can help children express concerns about their peer group or their appearance.

Judd's story

Puberty is really a confusing time. You're changing physically and emotionally. Every once in a while, my voice would crack. I'd wonder: "Geez, what's going on with my body? Am I sick?" It helped that my dad explained things to me. I usually walked around in an undershirt or without a shirt, and he could see the changes in my body. I grew hair on my chest and in my armpits. He told me that my body was changing and that I was growing into manhood.

He showed me his chest and said, "You can see that I have a hairy chest. You'll probably have a hairy chest, too." He explained that how the body is changing is just one step, and that we'd work on the emotional part, too. You know — how a man acts. How he holds himself. You can't act like an 8-year-old when you're a teenager.

Puberty is a new experience. You can't practice for it. The biggest thing for me is that my dad is a sounding board. We share experiences. I learned that the changes I was going through were normal.

My dad and I have always been able to talk. If I have questions about anything, I can go to him. When I started to grow hair on my face, he got all excited. It was a big "dad" moment.

"... my dad is a sounding board. We share experiences. I learned that the changes I was going through were normal."

Judd

He taught me how to shave. He loves showing me how to do things. If we weren't comfortable talking about everything else, that wouldn't have happened.

I started puberty when I was about 13 years old. My dad told me he was a slow developer, not beginning to change until he was about 15. He always said, "Don't make fun of people if they're slower to develop. It's just how their body works." When you're getting into the teen years, it's like O.K, I'm a man now, and you don't want guys teasing you that you're not a man yet.

Some parents may want to be very specific about worries common among adolescent boys. They include concerns about height, hair on their body, and the size of their penis. Parents can say: "Some young children begin to walk and talk earlier than others. Adolescents develop at different rates, too. Developing earlier or later than your peers doesn't mean there is anything wrong with you."

Another topic of concern to boys is nocturnal emissions or "wet dreams." Parents can prepare boys by telling them they may ejaculate in their sleep — that semen may come from their penis, and that it's a normal part of healthy development.

Children may also hear myths about the dangers of masturbation. It's important that children understand that touching themselves is safe and normal. In discussing this behavior with your children, it's key that you not shame them.

Dr. Rauch

Talking about your family's beliefs and values

FACT: In a survey of teens 88 percent said it would be easier to postpone sexual activity and avoid teen pregnancy if they were able to have more open, honest conversations about these topics with their parents.[5]

Most adults recall the first time they learned about sex. Sara was in the sixth grade when her friend asked her to explain a gesture a boy made during class. "She made a circle with fingers. Using her other hand, she put her finger into the circle." Sara instantly understood.

"Yuk!" she said. "Why would anyone stick their penis into a woman?" When Sara became a mom, she was determined that her son James would learn about sex from his parents, not from his friends on the playground. She also wanted James to understand that sexuality includes more than the physical act of sexual intercourse. It also includes values and emotions.

Sara and Mark believe there's no such thing as "the big talk." They believe that educating

Many young people say that what they're taught at home and at school, as well as their own personal values, influences their decision to postpone having intercourse.[6]

their son James about sexuality is a process.

They had their first talk with James about sexual intercourse when he was in elementary school. James had visited his aunt and read a book about how babies are made. When he came home that night, he wanted to share the book with his mom and dad. "Look!" he said, turning page after page. "This is how the sperm and the egg come together. It's called 'fertilization.' When I grow up, I get to make children!"

The book showed sexual intercourse between two people who were married. Being married before having sex was the same value James would learn in sexuality classes in middle school.

Sometimes James asked his parents questions about sex: "Do girls move a lot when they have sex?" "If you have one kid and want another, do you have to have sex again?"

As James grew up, Sara and Mark answered his questions. They were always careful to offer only what they thought he was ready to hear.

When James was 15 years old, he dated a girl in his class. One night, he walked into the kitchen and sat down with his mom and dad. "I used to think I'd wait 'til I was married to have sex," he said. "Now, I don't think I'll wait."

His dad was speechless. He thought that

James's comment meant he'd already had sex. But his mother knew from many conversations with her son that he hadn't. "I know there are things I have to be aware of," James said. "A girl can get pregnant..."

Sara interrupted her son. "It's not just about her getting pregnant, James," she said. "You risk getting a disease, too. When you decide to have sexual intercourse, consider all the consequences. Intercourse can change a relationship and dramatically change your life."

Intercourse can be a joyful and pleasurable experience. Telling James otherwise, his parents say, would be a lie.

Sara asked James to think about how he'd been raised: his parents were able to support him both emotionally and financially. "If you became a father now," she explained, "you'd have to make a lot of sacrifices to support your child." She also helped him consider how he'd feel marrying a woman he may not love.

James listened carefully. He agreed he wanted to take care of his children just as he'd been cared for. He wanted to provide for and spend time with them. For him, that meant waiting to have sex.

Sara and Mark told James that intercourse can be a joyful and pleasurable experience. Telling him otherwise, they say, would be a lie. They explained that they believe there is joy in sex only when people are committed to and respect each other in a long-term relationship.

As James left for college, his mom and dad reminded him about waiting to have sex. "You'll feel great desire for some of the young women you meet," Sara said. "I hope you'll remember the things we've talked about. Especially this: When someone says no, they mean no. Always show respect." One way to do that, she pointed out, is to talk with your partner before becoming physically intimate. It's the way to make sure you both want the same thing.

"If you are going to have sex," Mark reminded his son, "make sure you use a condom."

Sara and Mark marvel at how time has flown since their fourth grader came home delighted to know that he could "make children." They hope he remembers their many talks about their family's values and makes smart decisions.

Dr. Rauch

"They didn't shut down communication with anger or authoritarian dos and don'ts."

Consider This

Dr. Satcher: Sara and Mark have clearly created an environment where James could be comfortable talking with them. James knew he could trust his parents.

Dr. Rauch: They were in tune with James's questions at each stage of his development. They listened and used his questions as opportunities to discuss their family's values. They didn't shut down communication with anger or authoritarian dos and don'ts. This is often a challenge for parents when they're surprised by a child's questions or comments.

Dr. Satcher: Being controlling or coercive can backfire.

Dr. Rauch: A child may get angry and rebel to prove his independence from his parents. One way parents can create a warm, interactive environment that leads to the kinds of conversations James and his parents had is by spending unstructured time with their child.

Dr. Satcher: There's no substitute for spending time with your children. TV isn't a substitute. The computer isn't a substitute. Time together gives children the chance to open up and talk about difficult issues. Listening builds their self-esteem.

Dr. Rauch: Sara and Mark share with James their family's values. They want him to wait to have sexual intercourse. They know that he isn't ready to assume the responsibilities of parenthood. When parents help children think through the consequences of their actions, they're more likely to make safe decisions. One way to do this is to ask a child, "What do you think your life would be like if you were a dad now?" "How would you spend your time?" "I wonder what you would have to give up?"

Dr. Satcher

"There's no substitute for spending time with your children. TV isn't a substitute. The computer isn't a substitute."

Dr. Rauch

"Talking about the pleasures of sex is important, because it's the truth. If we aren't honest, we lose our credibility."

Dr. Satcher: Sara and Mark talk realistically with their son about sex. They point out potential consequences but acknowledge the pleasures of sex. This is important. And they're clear to point out that sex is fulfilling within a committed, monogamous, and enduring relationship.

Dr. Rauch: Our children are barraged with media messages about sex being pleasurable and desirable. But the media rarely portray that the most pleasurable sex happens within the context of a meaningful, long-term relationship. So parents need to be the source of this information. Talking about the pleasures of sex is important, because it's the truth. If we aren't honest, we lose our credibility.

Ask Yourself

- Do I understand the value of ongoing conversations with my child about sexuality, not just a "big talk" about the birds and the bees?

- Mark and Sara reacted calmly in conversations with their son. Do I react with shock or dismay when my child tells me upsetting news?

- Do I try to control my child's behavior? Or do I try to guide him by asking questions to help him think through the potential consequences of his actions?

- If I want my child to delay having sexual intercourse, do I emphasize the benefits of waiting as well as the potential physical and emotional consequences of intercourse?

- Am I honest with my child about the pleasures of sex when shared in a healthy relationship?

Remember

Parents can help young people who may be thinking about having sexual intercourse to consider the consequences of their decisions. Dr. Rauch suggests asking questions such as these: "What do you think your girlfriend will say to her friends about you if you've had sex with her?" "How do you think you will feel the next day, or the next week, when you see her?" "Will you continue to feel good?" "When you're thinking about being physically intimate with someone, ask yourself whether you'd trust her to keep your most personal secret. If not, are you sure you would trust her enough to have sex?" These types of questions, Dr. Rauch explains, can help young people consider the emotional impact of their decisions.

James's story

The conversations I had with my parents growing up were possible because we respect each other. We trust each other. We're loyal to each other. I know they love me. My parents are always supportive of me, regardless of the situation. That's helped me build a very strong foundation.

As I grew up, we decided together about my morals and ethics. I feel obligated to myself and to my parents to live by those morals. I can tell my parents anything, and they never get mad at me. They're sensitive and attentive to how I really feel about stuff. I don't have to worry about them talking down to me or treating me like some punk teen who needs a reality check.

When I'm attracted to a woman, sometimes I want to go beyond making out. That's where kids struggle. It's an ongoing battle between my morals and what I want emotionally and physically.

After a friend of mine had intercourse, he told me to wait. He and his girlfriend didn't have a very healthy relationship, and sex made it worse. He said he felt really awkward with her afterwards. But I have friends who have really good relationships with their girlfriends, and they have sex. They respect each other and

Teens who are "highly satisfied" with their relationship with their parents are nearly three times less likely to engage in sex than teens who experience "little satisfaction" with their parental relationships.[7]

agree on things. They're happy, so it makes me kind of jealous. I'd like to have a girlfriend. I feel ready to have someone to snuggle with and sleep with and to have a relationship. If it's working for these outstanding guys who have their heads on right, why shouldn't it work for me?

Sometimes I say, "Well, maybe having sex now would be O.K." That's where the conversations with my parents come in. I have a lot going for me. With all my goals and aspirations, I don't see having a baby. It's so far down the road. That's what really steers me away from sex. I keep telling myself that having sex is a huge risk, even with birth control pills and condoms. Nothing protects 100 percent.

If I did have sex, there might not be consequences, but I wouldn't know until it was too late. There are tons of other ways to be close. You can sleep together and not have sex — some of my friends do that. And you can make out. As long as the girl and the guy talk about it and agree, there are lots of ways to feel good, be intimate, and make your partner feel good without intercourse. That's where I am right now about sex.

Teens who wait to have sex say they feel more in control of their relationships and true to their moral or religious beliefs.[8]

Building trust with your child

Responding calmly to children's questions builds trust...

Many parents are caught off guard when their child asks questions about sexuality. Some admit they've laughed, quickly changed the subject, or simply said, *"What?"* When parents avoid kids' questions, or flat out lie, they lose the opportunity to give the facts and share their values. Still worse, their kids might get misinformation from their peers or elsewhere.

Responding calmly to children's questions builds trust and makes it more likely they'll bring you their questions and concerns. Donna found out that it's not always easy to answer a child's questions honestly.

Donna and her husband Jack know it's important to talk about sexuality with their kids. They look for opportunities, or teachable moments. But one morning, Donna was caught off guard.

Her son David was eating his cereal as he watched the news on TV. Suddenly, he said, "Mom, what's oral sex?"

Stunned, Donna looked at the 9-year-old. *I'm not ready for this*, she thought. She paused to collect herself and said, "It's when two people have sexual intercourse, and then talk about it."

David stared at her. "Oh, come on Mom!" he said.

Donna wasn't off the hook. She took a deep breath. "O.K.," she began again. "It's when a man puts his penis in a woman's mouth, and a man kisses a woman's vagina."

David was appalled. His face grew pale. "That's disgusting!" he said.

Donna tried to reassure him. "This is something some adults who love each other enjoy," she explained. "There will probably come a day when it doesn't seem disgusting to you." David went back to eating his cereal. Donna reminded him that he could always ask questions about things he doesn't understand. "If you ask your friends instead of me," she said, "you might not get the right information."

Donna realized the irony of her statement. "I had to tell him the truth," she said. "If I continued to make something up, he wouldn't come back to me. Then I'd lose those opportu-

> *"I had to tell David the truth. If I continued to make something up, he wouldn't come back to me."*
>
> Donna

Dr. Rauch

"It's important to think ahead about how you'll answer your child's questions about sexual intimacy."

nities to give him the information as I want him to hear it."

Donna is grateful for that day, because David has asked more questions. Donna tries to continue to be honest with him and give him the facts. "It helps build trust," she says.

Consider This

Dr. Satcher: I think Donna did a great job. At first, like a lot of parents, she was caught off guard. But I commend her for coming back with the correct information and being open and honest.

Dr. Rauch: It's important to think ahead about how you'll answer your child's questions about sexual intimacy. You can talk with your spouse or partner about how they'd handle certain questions. Friends are a great resource too, especially if they have older children. You can ask what they felt worked well in discussing sexuality, and what they wish they'd done differently.

Dr. Satcher: As children develop, there are natural opportunities to educate them about sexuality. They may raise questions about their own body or about something they hear on TV. Donna's honesty kept communication open with her son. She didn't react in a way that embarrassed him and may have shut down communication.

Dr. Rauch: If your child asks a question you're not prepared to answer, you can say, "That's an important question. I'd like some time to think about it." It's important to get back to your child with the correct information. If you don't know the answer, you can say, "I don't know. Let's find out." Then you can find the information together in a book, on the Internet, or from your pediatrician."

Dr. Satcher: Donna was comfortable using the correct terminology. When we call body parts by their real names, we let our children know we're being honest and trustworthy. Using madeup names sends the wrong message. It can give the impression that there's something shameful about their body.

Dr. Rauch: If your children know you're telling the truth, they'll continue to ask you questions. Parents need to set a tone that welcomes curiosity. When a child asks questions, you can say, "I love how you think. You always ask such great questions." You want to avoid reacting with shock: "Shame on you for asking such a question." Or, "Who told you that?" It's the tone as much as the words that keeps communication open.

Dr. Satcher

"When we call body parts by their real names, we let our children know we're being honest and trustworthy."

Ask Yourself

- If my child asked me a question and I didn't answer honestly, how could I bring up the subject later to give him the correct information?

- In what ways do I let my child know that his or her questions are always welcome?

- When talking about parts of the body, do I refer to them by their actual names or by nicknames?

Remember

When you tell your children the truth, they learn to trust you. Calling parts of the body their actual names is an example of telling the truth. When you do this, your child knows that you're willing to tell the truth. You're also teaching your child that his or her body is worthy of respect, not a source of shame. Practice saying the parts of the body out loud. That will make using the words with your child easier.

Mariama's story

Parents need to make sure their kids have accurate information about sexuality. That way the decisions their kids make are based on the facts.

Kids can tell when adults aren't telling the truth. When parents are uncomfortable with a subject, it comes through. Their kids won't go to them when they need someone to tell it to them straight. They'll turn to someone else. There are plenty of people who speak with confidence but have no idea what they're talking about.

Parents also need to share their own experiences with their kids. When it comes to sex, some parents get embarrassed. But when you can share your experiences — good and bad — children learn from you. Parents can teach their kids what to look for in a relationship. They can equip them to make good choices. They can help them avoid potentially abusive situations. When parents do this, their kids know they're trying to protect them.

I think it's hard for a lot of parents to talk with their kids honestly about sexuality, because they haven't really thought it through themselves. Maybe they don't even talk about

"When you can share your experiences — good and bad — children learn from you."

Mariama

it with their spouses or partners. But they still say to their kids, "I'm going to tell you what to do."

Talking about sexuality has to be a two-way dialogue or it will be a one-time talk. If you respect that your kids have opinions, they will be more open with you.

> *"Talking about sexuality has to be a two-way dialogue or it will be a one-time talk."*
>
> Mariama

I trust my parents to tell me the truth. Our conversations are always framed around how my choices will affect what I want to do with my life. They try to help me make my own choices. It's not: You *will* do this.

Sometimes I can have conversations with my parents. Sometimes I can't. So my parents encourage me to also talk with other adults we both trust. They've told these people "It's O.K. for you to talk with my daughter about these things."

Parents can't watch their children 24/7. So they have to tell them the truth, be willing to guide them, and then trust.

What's a period?

FACT: Girls are beginning to menstruate earlier now than in past generations.[10]

With so much information about sex in the media, parents often assume their children know how their body develops. Cindy didn't make that assumption. She wanted her daughter Polly to hear from her that as she reached puberty, her body would undergo dramatic changes. Getting her period was one important milestone.

Cindy wanted her girls to have positive feelings about every part of being a woman.

Raising three girls, Cindy talked with them often about puberty. She wanted to prepare them for how their body would change as they grew up. "When I was a girl," Cindy said, "menstruation was called 'The Curse.' But it's what makes us special." Cindy wanted her girls to have positive feelings about every part of being a woman.

As each of her girls began the fifth grade, Cindy found time to talk with them about changes in their body. Their talks included the topic of menstruation. "It's a sign that a girl is becoming physically mature," Cindy said. "It means your body is preparing for pregnancy." Cindy explained that with this came the

Polly and Cindy

responsibility not to get pregnant before they were ready to be a parent.

She explained that each month in a woman's body an egg travels through the fallopian tube to the uterus. The lining of the uterus has become thick and spongy with blood. After a sperm from a man fertilizes an egg, the egg attaches to the uterus. That's how a woman becomes pregnant. The uterus is the place in a woman's body where the baby grows and develops. "When an egg doesn't get fertilized, the lining of the uterus passes out of your body in your blood," she said. "When you bleed, it's called your period."

The day 13-year-old Polly got her period, Cindy congratulated her. "This is a wonderful step in your development," she said. "You're becoming a woman." Polly didn't share her mother's enthusiasm. "She cried," Cindy recalls. "She was so, so sad. I asked her why she was so upset."

"Doesn't this mean I'm going to have my period forever?" Polly asked. Cindy reassured her that a period lasts five to seven days. Then, it stops. She told her it doesn't return until the next month. Polly was relieved. Her tears stopped. "Well," Polly said with a smile, "maybe it will be O.K."

Cindy suggested that they tell Polly's dad she'd reached a new milestone. "I'll leave that up to you, Mom," Polly said.

Looking back, Cindy thinks she did a pretty good job of preparing her daughters for menstruation. What about Polly's concern she'd have her period 365 days a year? Cindy laughs, "I guess I left that part out."

Consider This

Dr. Satcher: Cindy did a good job preparing her daughter for her period. If girls are unprepared, it can be frightening. You can't always wait for children to bring up a topic. Sometimes they won't.

Dr. Rauch: Children develop at different rates, so parents can check with their pediatrician to find out when to talk about certain topics. Cindy was tuned in to her daughter and addressed menstruation at the right time. Parents have to be ready for these discussions earlier than they were 20 years ago. Ideally, parents would be well informed and comfortable discussing menstruation before their daughters turn 10.

Dr. Satcher: If you appear to be uncomfortable when your children ask questions about their bodies, you can shut down communication. It's best when parents bring up issues related to sexuality at appropriate times. It's really important that parents be well informed so they can teach their children and be good role models.

Dr. Satcher

"It's really important that parents be well informed so they can teach their children and be good role models."

Dr. Rauch: It was important that Cindy presented menstruation in a positive light. Some girls have mixed feelings about puberty. A parent can address this by saying, "Getting your period is an exciting time in your development. But learning to use tampons or sanitary napkins can be awkward. Sometimes when you have your period, you may have cramps. But many years from now, if you want to have a baby, you'll be glad your body works so well. Right now, though, it's an adjustment." You can also ask questions to uncover misconceptions: "Do you talk with your friends about having periods?" "What concerns do you have? I hope we can keep talking about how your body is changing."

Ask Yourself

- Do I watch for opportunities to discuss the physical and emotional changes my child is experiencing?

- Do I have the information I need to clearly and accurately explain those changes?

- Do I address any misconceptions she may have?

- How have I explained to my preadolescent or adolescent child that feeling awkward during adolescence is a natural part of growing up?

Remember

Mothers often take the lead in talking with their daughters about sexuality. Fathers have an important role, too. When fathers talk openly with their daughters about sexual health, their daughters are more likely to grow up to expect to talk openly with their partners. And girls who know that their fathers view them as competent and worthy of respect may be less likely to seek approval through sexual experiences with boys.[11]

Polly's story

In the fifth grade we had "Growing Up" groups. All the girls went into one room and talked to a counselor. Later, when my mom started talking to me about my period, I told her I already knew everything about it. It felt kind of weird hearing it from my mom.

The day I got my period, I was riding on my bike and I felt cramps. I contemplated not telling her, because my friends hadn't told their parents. I felt embarrassed, but I knew I could tell her, because we'd already talked about periods.

I told her, because I needed her advice. I cried. I didn't want to get my period. It seemed like such a hassle. I was in sports, and I didn't want having a period to interfere.

"Even if your children are embarrassed, explain what's happening in their body."

Polly

Talking with my mom was very comforting. She was really good at explaining things to me. It was a turning point for us. After that, talking with her about girl stuff and boys was easier.

Even if your children are embarrassed, explain what's happening in their body. It doesn't have to take long.

I'm glad my mom took the time to explain what was going on with my body. I don't know if I would have believed my friends. I've always thought my mom had the right information.

Issues of human sexuality are of enormous importance within families. How children are introduced to these topics — and by whom — can make a critical difference in how they view human sexuality and sexual relationships. It deeply affects their understanding of themselves as sexual beings. Parents who take the lead in talking about these issues can frame the discussion within their personal and religious values. Otherwise, people who have little respect for their family's view of life, and who may lack knowledge, might influence their children. Parents can also tell their children that there is no question about human sexuality they need be afraid, ashamed, or embarrassed to ask.

These discussions have never been easy for parents. But today, sexuality and eroticism pervade popular culture and the media. That's why having these conversations at appropriate times, in every stage of child development, is more important than ever.

Jon Fuller S.J., M.D., M.Div., Th.M.
Dr. Fuller is a Jesuit priest and an AIDS physician at Boston Medical Center.

Talking about relationships

FACT: A majority of parents of 8- to 12-year-olds say families don't talk enough about relationships and becoming sexually active.[12]

Parents who want their children to be sexually healthy teach them to build healthy relationships. The best relationships are based on friendship, trust, mutual respect, and the ability to communicate. When children learn this, they're more likely to grow up to have strong relationships with their friends, spouse or partner, and colleagues.

One morning Kris was reading the newspaper and eating breakfast with her daughters. "Listen to this," she said, quoting an advice column. "This girl's in love with a guy who's ignoring her, but she's never talked to him." Without showing her feelings about the story, Kris asked the girls their opinions. Eleven-year-old Shana said, "That's absurd. How can you be in love with someone you don't know or have never even talked to?"

Kris agreed. She used the opportunity to talk about love and relationships. "You may think you're in love and feel all tingling in your body," she explained. "But that's not love. Love is more than a pitter-patter feeling. It's more than liking how someone looks or the car they drive. Love is a very special feeling, and it's hard to describe."

Shana and Justine asked her to try. "What was it like for you, Mom?"

"I thought I was in love lots of times," Kris said. "But eventually, I learned what it really means." Love, she told her girls, is part of a meaningful relationship between two people. When two people are in love, they're kind to each other and enjoy being together.

"What was it about dad you loved?" Justine asked.

Kris explained there were lots of things. His qualities, she said, would help their love last forever. "I knew we shared values about raising kids and the sanctity of marriage. I knew he'd still love me if I got sick. And he's a good listener. Those things are important to me."

George has told his daughters what a good relationship means to him, too. "You want to be with someone who will be there through thick or thin," he says.

No relationship is perfect. Sometimes Kris and George argue. They say that's part of life.

By showing respect for your children and for other people, you teach your children the concept of respect.[13]

For example, one night company was coming. George called to say he'd be home "shortly." But when he arrived 30 minutes later, Kris was angry. And everyone knew it. "He didn't communicate well," she explained to her daughters. "He thought 30 minutes was 'shortly.' When you're in a relationship, it's important that you communicate well. My reaction didn't mean I don't love Daddy," she told her girls. "It meant I was mad at him."

Kris also gives positive examples. One time she was polishing her nails. George saw her struggling to apply polish to her left hand and offered to help. Shana and Justine were struck by his kindness. "That's an example of what someone does when he cares for you," Kris said.

Another time, a friend called to check on Justine, who had the flu. "That's a real friend," Kris said. "He's juggling a million things and still takes time to think about Justine. That's important not just with a life partner, but also with good friends."

Consider This

Dr. Satcher: This is proof that informed adults can serve as positive role models. Being a good role model is one of the most effective ways parents can teach their children about sexuality and responsibility.

Dr. Satcher

"Being a good role model is one of the most effective ways parents can teach their children about sexuality and responsibility."

Dr. Satcher

"...healthy relationships include shared values and beliefs about family and about life."

Dr. Rauch: Shana and Justine will have a sense of how caring adults show each other love and respect. They'll be more likely to grow up expecting to be treated that way.

Dr. Satcher: They'll understand that healthy relationships include shared values and beliefs about family and about life.

Dr. Rauch: Kris reminded Justine about her best friend's call when Justine was sick. That was a creative way to model what people in healthy relationships do for each other. This reminds us that parents can find positive role models outside the family for children to learn from too.

Dr. Satcher: As George points out, in healthy relationships people are committed to being there through thick and thin. Commitment builds over time. It takes more than two weeks or a month.

Dr. Rauch: Children also need to understand that no relationship is perfect. Kris teaches her daughters that people who love each other sometimes get angry at each other. It's important for children to see adults who've hurt someone's feelings admit it and then apologize.

Ask Yourself

- How would I describe to my child what it means to be in love?

- How do my relationships with friends, spouse, or partner model healthy or unhealthy relationships?

- When a friend or partner shows me respect, how can I point it out to my child as a positive example of friendship?

- Do I know adults outside our home who can be positive role models for my child?

- Do I teach my child that the healthiest relationships are based on friendship, trust, mutual respect, and the ability to communicate?

Remember

Children can learn about healthy relationships from a variety of sources: parents, mentors, favorite teachers, coaches, and youth leaders. When an adult is available through thick and thin the child learns that ongoing support can help them handle tough times.

Dr. Rauch

"...parents can find positive role models outside the family for children to learn from too."

Ernesto's story

"*It's second nature to me to treat women as equals and with respect, because that's what I saw growing up.*"

Ernesto

When I first met my girlfriend, there was no intention to be boyfriend and girlfriend. We just liked to share each other's time, tell each other what was going on, and make each other laugh. We went to the movies or bowling, or just talked on the phone, like I would with any of my friends.

We were best friends for a really long time, in teenage time. About a year or so. Eventually it was like: "Wow, I really like this person." Then we became girlfriend and boyfriend.

We can talk about anything — problems we had during the day and how happy we are to be in each other's company. As cheesy as it sounds, when I'm stressed out I can call her and feel better. It's always great to have that other person you can trust to be a shoulder to lean on.

I hear a lot of guys talk about women like "I'm going get some." You know, that whole state of mind where sex is all that matters and the person isn't even a person; where the heart doesn't even come into play.

It was important in my household to show respect to women. My father always showed respect to my mother, and she always taught us to do that. It's second nature to me to treat women as equals and with respect, because that's what I saw growing up.

At what age is it O.K. to have sex?

FACT: Only 23 percent of parents report they've talked with their children about when it may be appropriate to have a sexual relationship.[14]

"At what age is it O.K. to have sex?" is one of the most challenging questions a parent can be asked. The thought of your child having sex can be upsetting. As one teenager said, "That's the moment a parent realizes they aren't the main influence in their kid's life anymore." You may also worry about pregnancy and sexually transmitted infections.

Some parents tell their kids sex should be saved for marriage. Others, like Celia and Ted, believe their children will make the right choices if they help them talk through potential consequences of sexual intercourse and the benefits of waiting.

Celia's parents didn't talk with her about sex as she grew up. She wanted to raise her daughters differently. "I'm constantly looking for opportunities to bring up the subject," Celia says.

One day, 14-year-old Trish rushed into the house after school, dropped her backpack,

By their late teenage years, at least three-quarters of all teens have had intercourse.[15]

and said, "Hey, Mom. Know the hot news for the day? Two kids were caught behind the football field having sex. They got kicked out of school."

Trish was talking quickly, hardly taking a breath. "Why would anyone want to have sex in the woods?" she asked her mom. "It doesn't seem like a comfortable place. And they got caught, so obviously it wasn't a good place."

If the kids wanted to have sex, Celia asked her daughter, why do *you* think they would go to the woods?

Trish guessed they wanted a private place. Then she asked, "Where *do* kids have sex, since they live at home?"

Celia explained that kids who sneak around don't want parents to know what they're doing.

Celia knew this was the time to talk with Trish again about sexual intercourse. "If you have to sneak or hide, you aren't ready."

"Well, how do you know when you *are* ready?" Trish asked.

Celia was glad she and her husband Ted had planned for this talk with Trish. They had agreed not to give their children rules about when they could have sex. They didn't want to say that they'd be ready at a certain age.

In a survey of 2000 high school students, of those who'd had sexual intercourse, 91 percent had last done so in a home setting.[16]

Instead, they wanted their girls to know and respect themselves. Celia and Ted believed that's how their daughters could have healthy relationships. And that's how they would make good choices.

"First of all," Celia answered, "you might be ready when you care about someone you've been with a long time."

"What's a long time?" Trish asked.

"Well, it's not two months," Celia explained. "A long time is when you know someone in a lot of different ways: how they think, how they feel, and what they believe." She said that takes a long time.

"Well, at what age do you think sex *is* O.K.?" Trish pressed.

"I can't give an age," Celia explained. "It's not that simple. There's so much to consider: how you'd feel afterwards; whether you're being pressured; all those things."

Trish was listening carefully, so Celia kept talking. "I also believe it's important in a physical relationship that *both* people are satisfied, not just the guy. A couple is ready for sexual intercourse only after they've done other intimate things together and understand each other's bodies," Celia said.

Of teens who had experienced sexual intimacy, 47 percent said they had done something sexual or felt pressure to do something they weren't ready to do.[17]

"Sex in a relationship that is based on mutual respect will be pleasurable for both partners," Celia continued. "With all that to consider, it's important to talk about it together before having sex."

Trish said, "That's a good point."

Celia hopes their conversations show Trish that their family's values about sexual intimacy are different from those of the kids who had sex in the woods. Celia told Trish she hopes she talks with her when she feels she's ready for sexual intercourse.

Trish rolled her eyes. "Oh, Mom," she said. "I could just *imagine* telling you *that*."

Celia repeated a point she made earlier. "Well, I think that's one way you could know whether you're ready," she said. "When you're ready, you shouldn't need to hide it."

Trish thought about it. "Actually, that makes a lot of sense," she said.

Later, Trish heard a news report about a young woman who accused her sex partner of rape. "Obviously," Trish said, "they weren't talking with each other."

"I was glad to hear her say that," Celia says. "Her comment tells me she gets it."

Consider This

Dr. Rauch: When Trish asked her mom why someone would have sex in the woods, Celia listened calmly. That kept communication open. Celia was able to ask her daughter what *she* thought her peers might have been thinking. That led naturally into a great discussion about making good choices and having healthy relationships.

Dr. Satcher

Dr. Satcher: Celia also took the opportunity to reinforce their family's values about sexual intercourse: that choosing to be sexually active is a serious decision.

"It's parents' responsibility to talk with their children about the benefits of abstinence."

Dr. Rauch: Since Celia and Ted had discussed how they'd handle their daughter's questions about the subject, Celia was ready to share their views with Trish. When parents can have discussions together ahead of time, even if they're divorced, it's easier to be calm and clear when the opportunities arise to talk about their family's values with their children.

Dr: Satcher: It's parents' responsibility to talk with their children about the benefits of abstinence.

Dr. Rauch: It's important to discuss what abstinence means. Some children believe it means not having intercourse—but that oral sex is O.K. Other children think it means you can't kiss passionately. When parents are

Dr. Rauch

"When parents are encouraging abstinence, they need to be clear about what that means to each of them."

encouraging abstinence, they need to be clear about what that means to each of them.

Ask Yourself

- If my child asked me when it's O.K. to have sexual intercourse, how would I respond?

- Do I want my child's first sexual encounter to be different than my own? If so, how?

- How do I define abstinence?

- How would I know if my child were sexually active?

- How would I describe a "long-term" relationship to my child?

- Do the other important adults in my child's life and I agree on values about sexuality?

Remember

Most teens say it would be easier for young people to postpone intercourse if they had more open, honest conversations with parents about the topic. And most teens who already had sex said they wish they'd waited.[18] These facts underscore the importance of parents having ongoing, frank conversations about sexual health.

Francine's story

When I was 16, I dated a guy for six months and then we had sex. I thought it was the natural next step in the relationship. A month later we broke up.

The next week, at a school leadership conference, he hardly looked at me. I'd given my virginity to this guy, and he wouldn't acknowledge me. It was devastating.

I felt so rejected. I couldn't eat or sleep. My closest friends were supportive, but I didn't tell them I'd had sex. They were still virgins, and I didn't think they'd understand.

The only person I could turn to was my mom. I knew that she had to listen. We got along, but we'd never talked about sex and those kinds of things. She and my dad had gotten a divorce and she traveled for work. She was a single working mother. I'd sort of just stopped talking openly with her.

I was nervous. I didn't know how she'd react. I was afraid I'd be grounded. But I had to talk to someone.

One day, my mom and I were in the car. I asked her to pull over because I had to tell her something. She looked puzzled.

I blurted out, "Mom I had sex with him."

She started to cry, and that made me cry. She gave me a hug and told me she understood how I felt. That was the single most changing moment in our relationship. It was the first time I'd opened up and given her the chance to respond to something.

Don't get the wrong idea. She wasn't happy that I wasn't still a virgin. We talked about my relationship with the guy. He wasn't her favorite. And we talked about how great it was that my friends were supportive. My mom said she'd help me get through it.

Ever since that day, I've trusted my mom. Now we talk about everything. I don't make any big decision without bouncing it off her first.

I wish I'd told her before I had sex and not assumed she'd get mad. She's really wise. If we'd talked about it first, she might have encouraged me to wait.

I think parents need to check in on small topics like: "How was your day?" "What did you eat for lunch?" Then you can talk about the bigger questions: "How are you and your boyfriend doing?" "Are you guys serious about each other?"

I understand that a lot of parents are single parents. They're working hard and they're tired. But if your child doesn't feel that you care about the smaller things, there's no way they'll be honest with you about the bigger things.

"If your child doesn't feel that you care about the smaller things, there's no way they'll be honest with you about the bigger things."

Francine

I recently read a quote by Dr. Martin Luther King, Jr.: "Our lives begin to end the day we become silent about things that matter."

As a pastor, father, and grandfather, I believe we have a fundamental responsibility to adequately prepare young men and women to make wise decisions as spiritual and sexual beings. We must be participants in efforts that strengthen values of trust, self-love, self-respect, discipline, and patience in our youth. And that starts at home.

For eight years, the Black Church Initiative of the Religious Coalition for Reproductive Choice has informed and encouraged African American families and ministries to break the silence around issues related to sex and sexuality. By improving and increasing communication between teens and their parents, guardians, or caregivers, we are able to build stronger relationships, healthier communities, and a lasting legacy.

We cannot remain silent and closed-minded. Until we realize that, young people will continue to engage in risky sexual behavior, babies will continue to have babies, children will continue to be exposed to syphilis and HIV.

Honest conversations must take place at the kitchen table and in the family room. That will improve the quality of life for all God's children.

Reverend Carlton W. Veazey
President, Religious Coalition for Reproductive Choice

Oral sex and teens

FACT: 58 percent of 10- to 12-year-olds surveyed want to know more about dealing with peer pressure to have sex.[19]

"So many kids don't think oral sex is sex. They just think it's part of making out."

Melanie

Oral sex was once considered the most intimate of sexual acts. Now children report that many of their classmates casually engage in oral sex, sometimes with people they hardly know. Some children are responding to social pressures. They think that participating in oral sex will make them more popular. Others wrongly believe it's a "safe" alternative to vaginal intercourse.

Parents are shocked to learn that oral sex is so prevalent among young people. It's difficult enough for many adults to talk with their spouses or partners about oral sex, much less their children. But when so many young people believe that oral sex isn't sex, it's important that parents find ways to talk with them about it.

Connie makes sure that she and her daughter Melanie, a senior in high school, spend time together. They exercise, go to the movies, or shop at the mall. While they're hanging out, Connie talks often with her mom about kids who are having sex. Many times the topic is oral sex. "So many kids don't think oral sex is sex," Melanie says. "They just think it's part of making out. But I think it *is* sex."

Connie is glad Melanie believes that oral sex is sex. "After all," Connie says, "it's a very intimate act. And when you have oral sex, you also risk getting a disease."

They first discussed oral sex a few years ago, after something happened at the middle school. Connie's friend who taught at the school called with a shocking story. A group of eighth graders were seen behind the school. Six girls were performing oral sex on six boys. "They were learning about oral sex," Connie says, "like we learned to French kiss!"

Connie hung up the phone as Melanie ran into the house. "Mom, you won't believe this!" Connie told her she'd already heard.

"They're only 13 years old!" Melanie said. "And they've done it before!"

Melanie said that maybe the reason the girls did that was to get the guys to like them.

Connie explained that oral sex can feel good but has no place outside a committed relationship. Oral sex is sex. Kids who act as if it's no big deal aren't ready for it.

"Those girls have ruined their reputations,"

> *"It's a very intimate act. And when you have oral sex, you risk getting a disease."*
>
> Connie

Dr. Satcher

"Oral sex carries the risk of sexually transmitted diseases, including human papillomavirus, herpes and chlamydia."

Melanie added. "The whole town knows about it. They'll live with that forever."

Connie and her daughter talked about the double standard often attached to sexual intimacy: girls who have sex are sometimes called "promiscuous," but guys who have sex are called "studs."

"That's true," Melanie complained, "but it's not fair."

Connie was relieved to hear that her values and her daughter's were the same. She was more determined than ever to keep communication with her daughter open and frank.

Consider This

Dr. Rauch: The trend toward girls performing oral sex on boys is troubling but all too common. It's not an easy subject to talk about. Both Melanie and her mom trusted each other enough to talk about what had happened. That trust was built over time. Since they'd discussed oral sex before, they were able to talk about what's often an uncomfortable subject.

Dr. Satcher: As Connie said, oral sex is sex. Children often think oral sex is safe. It isn't safe. It carries the risk of sexually transmitted diseases, including human papillomavirus, herpes and chlamydia. It's an intimate act and, therefore, should be treated as such.

Dr. Rauch: Some adolescent girls view oral sex as no big deal and even feel as if it gives them a sense of power. Connie did well to underscore that, in this situation, oral sex was not the sign of an intimate, loving relationship. As parents, we need to help children understand that sexual intimacy isn't just about physical sensations. It's also about emotions. Sexual intimacy is most satisfying when it's mutually pleasurable and part of a meaningful, respectful relationship.

Dr. Satcher: Anything that suggests that young people aren't taking sex seriously or they are taking it as a game is troubling. It belittles sexuality. And it says something about the child's self-concept.

Dr. Rauch: It's important that parents help their child realize that what feels good physically in the moment may have upsetting consequences. Melanie said the girls ruined their reputations. Connie could have said, "I wonder what it'll be like for the girls to see the guys walking down the hallway, or with other girls?" "How do you think these boys and girls will feel knowing that their classmates, teachers, and coaches will know about this?" "I wonder why the girls *did* perform oral sex?" These conversations can help teens consider how they'd handle situations themselves.

Dr. Rauch

"...we need to help children understand that sexual intimacy isn't just about physical sensations. It's also about emotions."

Ask Yourself

- If my child asked me whether oral sex is considered sex, how would I answer?

- What steps can I take to make sure I'm knowledgeable when talking with my child about oral sex?

- Have I discussed with my child that there's often a double standard as it relates to boys and girls being sexually intimate?

- How would I explain this statement: Sexual intimacy is satisfying when it's pleasurable to both people and occurs as part of a long-term, committed, and monogamous relationship.

Remember

One way to talk about this subject with your child is to say you've read stories that say some young people are engaging in oral sex. You could ask: "Do you know what oral sex is?" "When do you think it's appropriate to engage in oral sex?" If your child doesn't want to talk about it, you can say: "Sometimes it's awkward to talk about these subjects, but I want you to have correct information." By talking with other adults about the trend of young people engaging in oral sex, you can become more comfortable discussing the subject, and be better prepared to answer your child's questions.

Alex's story

I think a lot of girls perform oral sex because they don't want to have intercourse, and they feel obligated to do something. But oral sex isn't something to be expected. If people have oral sex, it should be a mutual desire.

Oral sex is an intimate act. Both the man and woman deserve to have control. No one should have oral sex because they feel like they have to, to be more popular, or to keep a partner.

A lot of people are afraid to teach sex education in the schools, because they think it promotes sexual activity. But kids are curious. They think about sex. A lot of kids are already

having sex, including oral sex. Oral sex can be risky. Diseases can be transmitted through oral sex. So I think it's important to teach kids in school about oral sex and about mutual respect.

Sexually transmitted infections

There are many sexually transmitted infections (STIs) — sometimes also called sexually transmitted diseases (STDs).

Many STIs increase a person's risk for infection with HIV.

Here are basic facts about some of the most common STIs.[20, 21] To learn more about these STIs and others, visit www.plannedparenthood.org or call the CDC National Sexually Transmitted Diseases Hotline 800-227-8922.

Chlamydia

Chlamydia is a curable infection caused by bacteria. Untreated, it can lead to infertility in men and women. In women, chlamydia can cause pelvic inflammatory disease (PID). (see below for PID)

Transmission: Vaginal and anal intercourse, oral sex.

Symptoms: 75 percent of women and 25 percent of men experience no symptoms and don't know they have the infection, but can infect sexual partners. When symptoms are present, they can include discharge from the vagina or penis, a burning sensation when urinating, more frequent urination, abdominal pain and/or low back pain, nausea, fever, pain during intercourse, bleeding between menstrual periods, swelling, or pain in the testicles.

Prevention: Avoid vaginal and anal intercourse and oral sex. Latex condoms used perfectly may reduce the risk of infection.[22]

Pelvic Inflammatory Disease (PID)

Pelvic inflammatory disease (PID) is most often a complication of untreated chlamydia and gonorrhea. It's an infection that harms a woman's reproductive system. It involves the uterus, the lining of the uterus, the fallopian tubes and the ovaries. Scarring in the cavity near a woman's reproductive organs can cause chronic pain. These infections can also cause scar tissue that blocks the fallopian tubes. If both tubes are completely blocked, a woman is infertile. If the tubes are partially blocked, a woman can experience a tubal pregnancy. When a tubal pregnancy is not treated, it can cause death.

Transmission: Vaginal intercourse.

Symptoms: Common symptoms include unusually long or painful menstrual periods, vaginal discharge, pain in the lower back and abdomen, and pain during intercourse.

Prevention: Avoid vaginal intercourse. Latex condoms used perfectly may reduce the risk of infections that if untreated can lead to PID.[22]

Trichomoniasis

Trichomoniasis is a condition caused by a parasite. It's a common cause of vaginal infection.

Transmission: Vaginal intercourse.

Symptoms: Sometimes women have no symptoms. When symptoms are present, they may include a discharge with an unpleasant odor, blood in the discharge, itching in and around the vagina, swelling in the groin, and frequent urination. During pregnancy, it can cause early termination of pregnancy and premature birth. Men rarely have symptoms.

Prevention: Avoid vaginal intercourse. Latex condoms used perfectly may reduce the risk of infection.[22]

Genital herpes (HSV-1 and HSV-2)

Genital herpes is caused by Herpes Simplex Viruses (HSV) type 1 (HSV-1) and type 2 (HSV-2). Most genital herpes is caused by HSV-2. HSV-1 also causes genital herpes, but more commonly causes "cold sores" on the mouth and lips. Of all genital herpes diagnosed in adolescents, one-third are the result of HSV-1 transmission through oral sex.[23] There is no cure. Medication is available to reduce the frequency of recurrences, relieve symptoms, and make it less likely a person will infect his or her partner.

Transmission: By touching the genitals and through sexual intimacy including kissing, vaginal and anal intercourse, and oral sex. HSV can be spread to a baby during childbirth.

Symptoms: Many people with genital herpes have no symptoms. Symptoms may include itchy, painful blisters in the genital area or around the mouth. These blisters may last a few days or more than a week. The virus stays in the body. A person with no visible sores can still transmit the virus to a partner.

Prevention: Avoid vaginal and anal intercourse and oral sex. During an outbreak, refrain from sexual intimacy until sores are healed. Between outbreaks, latex condoms used perfectly may reduce the risk of infection.[22] Medication that suppresses the virus can reduce the risk of transmission.[24] Cesarean section reduces transmission during childbirth.[25]

Gonorrhea

Gonorrhea is a curable infection caused by bacteria.

Transmission: Vaginal and anal intercourse and oral sex. It can also be spread to a baby during childbirth.

Symptoms: Men usually experience a burning feeling and a white or yellow discharge from their penis. Women can experience burning and a discharge from the vagina, but often show no symptoms or minor symptoms, which can be mistaken for a bladder or vaginal infection. Untreated, gonorrhea can cause PID.

Prevention: Avoid vaginal and anal intercourse and oral sex. Latex condoms used perfectly significantly reduce the risk of transmission of gonorrhea in men and may reduce the risk of transmission in women.[22]

Hepatitis B Virus (HBV) infection

Hepatitis B infection is caused by a virus. Some people's body gets rid of the virus naturally. In others it remains for life. In those infected for life, the virus can cause liver cancer.

Transmission: Vaginal and anal intercourse, oral sex, or by sharing unclean needles. HBV can be spread to a baby during childbirth. Experts say all body fluids, including saliva, should be considered to be infectious.

Symptoms: About 30 percent of persons infected with HBV have no visible symptoms. When symptoms are present, they may include extreme fatigue, abdominal pain, loss of appetite, nausea, vomiting, joint pain and, later, yellowing of the skin and of the white part of the eye.

Prevention: Avoid vaginal and anal intercourse and oral sex. Avoid sharing needles. Latex condoms used perfectly may offer some protection.[22] Children and adults free of HBV infection can receive a series of HBV vaccinations. This vaccine will prevent hepatitis caused by HBV.

Human papillomavirus (HPV) infection

There are three kinds of HPVs, two of which can infect the reproductive tract. One kind causes genital warts; the other kind is associated with cervical cancer and cancers of the penis or anus.

Transmission: The kinds of HPVs that infect the genital area are transmitted primarily through vaginal and anal intercourse and oral sex.

Symptoms: Genital warts, especially on the penis, are often so small they cannot be seen. When warts are visible, they usually appear as a raised, flesh-colored growth. Sometimes they itch. A person can have one episode or recurrent outbreaks of genital warts.

Cancer-causing HPVs: The body is usually able to get rid of HPV naturally. In the unusual case where the HPV persists, it can increase a woman's risk of cervical cancer. Pap tests can detect early, pre-cancerous conditions of the cervix, which are easily cured.[26] Cancer of the penis is rare. Anal cancer can be diagnosed with a Pap test.[27]

Prevention: Avoid vaginal and anal intercourse and oral sex. Latex condoms used perfectly may reduce the risk of infection and disease,[22] but more studies are needed. The virus may exist in areas not covered by the condom.

Human Immunodeficiency Virus infection (HIV)

Infection with HIV is not curable. The virus weakens the immune system and causes Acquired Immune Deficiency Syndrome (AIDS), a life-threatening illness.

Transmission: The virus can be present in blood, semen, vaginal fluids, and breast milk. It can be passed between persons during vaginal and anal intercourse and less commonly through oral sex. It can also be spread by sharing unclean needles and during pregnancy, childbirth, and breastfeeding.

Symptoms: During the first few weeks after HIV infection, most people have severe flu-like symptoms that may last a few days or a couple of weeks. After this, they may remain without symptoms for years. When HIV has significantly weakened the immune system, the body is vulnerable to life-threatening infections. The symptoms vary from rapid weight loss to diarrhea, fatigue, and night sweats.

Prevention: Avoid vaginal and anal intercourse. Latex condoms used perfectly offer excellent protection against the transmission of HIV during vaginal intercourse.[22] Avoid sharing needles. There are medications that are effective for preventing transmission to babies at childbirth. Many STIs increase a person's risk for infection with HIV.

Syphilis

Syphilis is a curable infection caused by bacteria.

Transmission: Vaginal and anal intercourse or oral sex. Syphilis can be transmitted to an unborn baby during pregnancy. Syphilis is passed through direct contact with syphilis sores or ulcers. Sores can occur on the external genitals, vagina, anus, or in the rectum, on the lips, and in the mouth.

Symptoms: There are three stages of syphilis. Primary syphilis occurs immediately after infection. A painless sore is present, usually on the genitals. Because the sores aren't painful, persons may not know they are infected.

Several weeks later, the sore heals. Within a short period of time, a skin rash appears, usually on the hands or soles of the feet. A person may also experience fatigue, muscle pain, and hair loss. In the latent stage, a person might have no symptoms while brain and heart damage occurs. Untreated syphilis may cause irreversible brain damage and/or death.

Prevention: Avoid vaginal and anal intercourse and oral sex. Latex condoms used perfectly provide significant protection when they prevent contact with infected areas.[22]

NOTE: Perfect condom use means using condoms consistently and correctly.

Prevention recomendations with respect to condom use (pp. 63-67) are taken from the National Institutes of Health's *Workshop Summary: Scientific Evidence on Condom Effectiveness for Sexually Transmitted Disease (STD) Prevention.* (see endnote 22 or visit www.niaid.nih.gov/dmid/stds/condomreport.pdf)

Beginning to use birth control

FACT: When mothers talk with young people about sexuality, and their conversations include topics such as birth control, condoms, and reproduction, those young people are more likely to delay sexual intercourse and use protection when they do have sex.[29]

From half to three-quarters of sexually experienced 12- to 14-year olds said they used contraception the first time they had sex.[28]

Some parents worry that by talking with their kids about birth control they're giving them permission to have sex. But approximately half of all teens have sex by the time they leave high school.

Each year approximately one million U.S. teens become pregnant,[30] and millions contract a sexually transmitted infection.[31]

Dawn and Todd are confident that talking with their daughter about contraception—and their values about sexual intimacy—will help protect her from unintended pregnancy and infections.

Gina, the 15-year-old daughter of Dawn and Todd, was dating a 17-year-old guy. Her parents had often talked with Gina about the reasons for waiting to have sexual intercourse. "When you do have sex," Dawn said, "we hope you'll be in a relationship with someone you truly can trust — someone you feel committed to. And we hope it's a monogamous relationship — that you're both monogamous."

Dawn and Todd know that some young people think they're being monogamous when they have only one sex partner for a mere few weeks. They explained that, to them, being monogamous means being faithful to someone you know well. And that it's impossible to know someone well after a short time.

They also discussed the physical and emotional risks of having sex when you're very young. "Most teens can't handle all the emotions that come with having sexual intercourse," Todd told his daughter.

"You have a bright future," Dawn explained. "Pregnancy or illness would change your life forever. No protection works 100 percent."

Despite their wishes, Dawn and Todd knew that Gina might not wait to have sex. "Abstinence is a great idea," Dawn says. "We were going to do everything possible to encourage her to wait, but we also had to be realistic: a lot of Gina's friends were having sex."

Sometimes Dawn asked Gina, "Honey, do you and Frankie ever talk about having sex?"

Gina was horrified. "Mom!" she said. "We aren't going to do *that!*"

Fifteen- to 24-year-olds represent one-quarter of sexually experienced Americans, but account for half of the newly diag-nosed sexually transmitted infections.[32]

About one in six teenage women practicing contraception combine two methods, primarily the condom and another method.[33]

Dawn reminded Gina that her job as a mother is to keep her daughter safe. "If you start talking about it," she said, "please tell me. You need to protect yourself with birth control *and* condoms."

After Gina and Frankie had been dating for more than a year, she told her mom that a friend had started to have sex. Dawn asked, "Gina, have you and Frankie talked about having sex?" This time, Gina said yes.

"If there's a chance you'll have intercourse," Dawn said, "it's important to be responsible." Gina agreed to go to the doctor for birth control pills.

After Gina's appointment, Dawn and the doctor talked. "I can't reveal what we discussed," the doctor said. "But you did the right thing." Driving home, Gina thanked her mom for making the appointment with the doctor.

"I'm glad Gina told me she might have sex," Dawn says. "I didn't agree with her decision. But knew I couldn't change her mind. I didn't want to risk pushing her away. I cherished being able to talk so openly with her. All I can do now is make sure we keep talking—and keep encouraging Gina to be as safe as possible."

Consider This

Dr. Rauch: Dawn is right on target. It's important to talk with children about the benefits of waiting to have sex in the context of our hopes for their future. For example, "I hope you can go to college, have a family, and a satisfying career." The many conversations Todd and Dawn had with their daughter made it possible for her to tell them the truth, even when it wasn't what they wanted to hear.

Dr. Satcher: Most parents prefer that their daughters wait until they're in mature, enduring, monogamous relationships to have sexual intercourse. But we don't understand all of the reasons some people choose to become sexually active. So we have to make sure that young people have information about contraception and condoms, and access to that protection, if they choose to have sex.

Dr. Rauch: Some parents think that it's confusing to encourage children to wait to have intercourse and also teach them about protection. Adolescents *can* hear those messages side by side. Parents could say, "I'm glad you told me the truth. We've talked about the reasons to wait. Sex can complicate a relationship. Neither the pill nor condoms offer 100 percent protection. Pregnancy or disease would alter your life forever. But I want you to be as safe as possible." It's also important for parents

About 40 percent of American women become pregnant before the age of 20.[34]

to clearly express their values. For example, "My talking to you about the safest ways to have sex doesn't mean that I think you're ready. It means that I realize you'll make your own decision. If you decide to have sex, I want you to be as safe as possible."

Dr. Satcher: That's an appropriate message.

Dr. Rauch: When parents learn that a child is considering having sex, they can help her think it through. They can say: "Let's talk about whether taking birth control pills is really the best choice for you. If you believe you're ready for sexual intercourse, you need to know how to protect yourself. Do you think having birth control pills may make it more difficult for you to say no when you don't want to have sex? Remember, birth control pills don't protect against sexually transmitted infections. I hope you and your partner have talked about using latex condoms, too."

Dr. Satcher: When you encourage your daughter to share how she feels, you're showing that you're interested in her, and that she's important and special. Children who feel valued are more likely to make healthy choices. Research shows that children who get open and honest messages from their parents are more likely to postpone sexual intercourse than those who don't get the information they need. Moreover,

"Research shows that children who get open and honest messages from their parents are more likely to postpone sexual intercourse than those who don't get the information they need."

Dr. Satcher

they're more likely to use contraception if they do have sex.

Dr. Rauch: Arranging for Gina to see the doctor didn't mean they supported her decision to become sexually active. It meant they loved her and wanted to help protect her.

Ask Yourself

• If my daughter asked me to take her to the doctor for birth control, how would I respond?

• Do I hesitate to have conversations about sex and contraception with my child? If so, why?

• When discussing birth control with my child, do I also emphasize the importance of using latex condoms perfectly — consistently and correctly — to help protect against infection?

• In what ways do I let my child know that she or he can talk honestly with me without having to worry about being criticized?

Remember

Even though Dawn didn't agree with her daughter's decision to have sex, she helped her get birth control. As children grow up, they make more decisions on their own. Though often difficult to accept, this is a natural and healthy part of growing up. Children are more likely to make healthy choices if you continue to share your values with them, and equip them with information and a sense of self-worth.

Talking with children about sexual intimacy

Parents can help young people who may be thinking about having sexual intercourse consider the consequences of their decisions. Dr. Rauch suggests asking questions such as these:

"What do you think your girlfriend will say to her friends about you if you've had sex with her?"

"How do you think you will feel the next day, or the next week, when you see her? Will you continue to feel good?"

"When you're thinking about being physically intimate with someone, ask yourself whether you'd trust her to keep your most personal secret. If not, are you sure you would trust her enough to have sex with her?"

Dr. Rauch explains that these types of questions can help young people consider the emotional impact of their decisions.

Vanessa's story

When I was 19 I'd just started to have sex with my boyfriend. We'd talked about our decision and agreed to use condoms and birth control. I wanted to tell my mom because there are very few things that I don't share with her.

I wondered how I was going to tell her this. I was wringing my hands. Even if she told me to not have sex, I knew I would anyway. But I wanted to discuss birth control and other things with my mom. When I told her, the car swerved. She was kind of upset. You know, scared that I'd get pregnant and have to drop out of school. I think she realized that I wasn't her little girl anymore.

Some of my friends were always criticized by their parents. They were very self-conscious. Neither my mom nor my dad were ever judgmental or critical.

My mom arranged for me to go to the doctor to talk about birth control. Even if I was on the pill, she said she wanted me to protect myself with condoms. I would tell my child the same thing. You don't really know where someone else has been. The person you're with might not even know if he has an STD.

I'm so glad I can talk with my mom. Any time you share something with a friend or a parent, you feel better. So, if your parents are clued in to what you're doing, and you can talk with them, you have someone who's smart about these things. They can give you advice. My mom's knowledgeable about health — not just sexual health. I could go to her if I had a lump in my breast or irregular bleeding.

If I couldn't talk to my mom about these things, I don't know who I'd ask. I need someone to turn to who has more experience than me. Someone who has my best interest at heart. For me, that's my mom.

It is crucial that families cultivate a positive attitude toward sexuality and an openness when talking about sexual health. This is the central legacy of Jewish sexual tradition. The Biblical Priests, and later the Rabbis, spoke openly about sex and sexual health. There was no shame in speaking of sexual urges, ejaculation, menstruation, masturbation, and intercourse. This responsibility has transferred, in large part, to parents. When we are silent about these topics, ignorance and fear results. This leaves our children vulnerable to infection and disease. Parents can protect their children by speaking candidly with them about sexual health in ways that are loving, emotionally sensitive, and developmentally appropriate.

Rabbi Sara Paasche-Orlow
Hebrew Rehabilitation Center for the Aged
Boston, Massachusetts

Methods of birth control

If young people decide to have sexual intercourse it's important that they use latex condoms perfectly — consistently and correctly — with another method of birth control. The other methods of birth control don't reduce the risk of STIs.

Selecting the right method of birth control can be a complicated process. Young people who can talk with a trusted and informed adult are more likely to make good choices.

It's important to visit a health care provider for specific instructions about the use of birth control before engaging in sexual intercourse. Unfortunately this often doesn't happen. The following is basic information about various methods of birth control. For more complete information, visit www.plannedparenthood.org or the contraceptive choices section of www.managingcontraception.com.

Continuous Abstinence
When a person continuously abstains from sexual intercourse, pregnancy is not possible because the egg and sperm don't join.

Effectiveness in preventing pregnancy: 100 percent unless a woman is forced to have intercourse or changes her mind.

Oral Contraceptives
Combined birth control pills contain two hormones — an estrogen and a progestin — which block the release of eggs from the ovaries and thicken the mucus to prevent sperm from joining with an egg. Progestin-only pills are also available. They thicken cervical mucus to prevent the egg and sperm from joining, and may stop ovulation. Extended or continuous use of combined birth control pills is an option. Instead of taking pills for 21 days — followed by seven hormone-free days — a woman takes combined pills for several months before having a hormone-free interval.[35, 36]

Effectiveness in preventing pregnancy: 92 percent to 99.7 percent depending on how perfectly they're used. [37]

Contraceptive Shots

Hormone shots stop the release of eggs in a woman's body. In some women, shots thicken the mucus in the cervix to prevent the sperm from joining the egg. Shots are administered every three months. When a woman stops having shots, her body eventually begins to release eggs again, and she can become pregnant. [35, 36]

Effectiveness in preventing pregnancy: Between 97 percent and 99.7 percent, depending on how perfectly they're used. [37]

Intrauterine Device (IUD)

An IUD is a T-shaped plastic device that releases copper or a progestin. It is placed into the uterus. The IUD remains effective as a contraceptive for years. Once the IUD is removed, the contraceptive effect is immediately reversed. For various health reasons, it is recommended that women at high risk for sexually transmitted infections not use an IUD. [35, 36] Some healthcare experts recommend against IUD use in some teens.

Effectiveness in preventing pregnancy: 99 percent to 99.9 percent. [37]

The Patch

A thin plastic patch that contains hormones, is worn on the skin, and releases hormones into the bloodstream to prevent the ovaries from releasing an egg. It also thickens cervical mucus to prevent sperm from joining with the egg. [35, 36]

Effectiveness in preventing pregnancy: 92 percent to 99.7 percent depending on how perfectly it's used. [37]

The Ring

A flexible ring placed inside the vagina, near the cervix, releases hormones. It works by usually preventing the ovaries from releasing an egg, and by sometimes thickening the cervical mucus to prevent sperm from joining the egg.[35, 36]

Effectiveness in preventing pregnancy: 98 percent to 99.7 percent depending on how perfectly it's used.[37]

Cervical Cap

The cervical cap is thimble-size cup which is placed inside the vagina before sexual intercourse to cover the cervix. Before inserting it, a gel or foam spermicide is placed inside the cap. Spermicides block and kill sperm. The cap keeps sperm from reaching the egg.[35, 36]

Effectiveness in preventing pregnancy: 84 percent to 91 percent for women who've not had a child, and 68 percent to 74 percent for women who've had a child, depending on how perfectly it's used.[37]

Diaphragm

The diaphragm is a shallow latex cup that's placed inside the vagina before sexual intercourse to cover the cervix. Before inserting it, a gel or foam spermicide is placed inside the diaphragm. Spermicides block and kill sperm. The diaphragm keeps sperm from reaching the egg.[35, 36]

Effectiveness in preventing pregnancy: 84 percent to 94 percent depending on how perfectly it's used.[37]

Condoms for Men

The condom is a thin cover for the penis that stops sperm from reaching the egg. Condoms are made from latex (rubber), lambskin or polyurethane. Latex condoms are considered to be most effective. Most studies about the effectiveness of condoms in preventing pregnancy and HIV have been conducted on latex condoms. Lambskin condoms can prevent pregnancy but may permit HIV, the hepatitis B virus, and the herpes simplex virus to pass through microscopic pores. Polyurethane condoms have not been studied as extensively for their effectiveness in preventing the spread of sexually transmitted infections.

With latex condoms use only water-based lubricants. (see p. 89: How to use a condom correctly) Latex condoms packaged with a spermicide on the inside and the outside of the condom are no longer recommended. A spermicidal foam, gel, or film may be inserted into the vagina before intercourse to increase the condom's effectiveness in preventing pregnancy.[35, 36]

Effectiveness of latex condoms in preventing pregnancy: 85 percent to 98 percent depending on how perfectly they're used.[37, 38]

Condoms for Women
The polyurethane condom for women is a pouch with flexible rings at both ends. It is inserted into the vagina to keep sperm from joining an egg.[35, 36]

Effectiveness in preventing pregnancy: 79 percent to 95 percent depending on how perfectly they are used.[37]

Emergency Contraception
Emergency contraceptive pills are hormone pills taken within 120 hours of unprotected or inadequately protected intercourse. Using emergency contraceptive pills is not as effective as using a regular method of birth control to prevent pregnancy. As another method of emergency contraception, a copper IUD may be inserted into a woman's uterus for five to eight days following unprotected or inadequately protected intercourse.[35, 36]

Effectiveness in preventing pregnancy: The earlier emergency contraceptive pills are taken after unprotected or inadequately protected intercourse, the more effective they are. Emergency contraceptive pills do not work if a woman is already pregnant. Nor do they harm the pregnancy if a woman is already pregnant. Insertion of an IUD after unprotected or inadequately protected intercourse is more effective than emergency contraceptive pills.[37] Some health experts recommend against IUD use in some teens

Condoms

FACT: More than eight in ten parents say children should be taught how to use condoms.[39]

Latex condoms used perfectly — consistently and correctly — are highly effective in preventing pregnancy and HIV.[40, 41] More studies are needed to measure their effectiveness in preventing other STIs.

Young people who have talked about condoms with a parent before having sexual intercourse for the first time are three times more likely to use condoms during that first experience than children who haven't had those talks. These children are also 20 times more likely to continue to use condoms in the future.[42]

Margie and Jay wanted to be sure their son knew, that if he had intercourse, using a condom was essential.

Margie and Jay talked often with their adolescent son about sex, and reminded him of the importance of using a condom to protect himself and his partner if he had intercourse. They also gave him a strong message: they wanted him to wait to have sex. "It's about safety,"

Twenty-five percent of teens surveyed say they need more information on how to use condoms.[43]

they told him. "Both emotional and physical." Margie and Jay believe that when children are told not to do something, they want more than ever to try it. So as Sam grew up, they talked about a lot of subjects ranging from responsibilities to relationships. They told Sam that his body would be ready to have sex before he would be emotionally ready.

Margie knew it was important to talk about sex in positive terms, but also to talk about potential consequences.

One day Margie put a few latex condoms in the bathroom cabinet. "Right next to the aspirin and shaving lotion," she says. "That was my way of saying condoms are part of every day life. Nothing to be squeamish about."

It was important to talk about sex in positive terms, but also to talk about potential consequences. "Sex between people who are mature and responsible is pleasurable and fulfilling," Jay told him. "There are no feelings of shame. But if you aren't ready to handle sex, it can create heartache."

Jay went on to explain some of the possible consequences. "People can feel jealous or possessive," he said. "And sometimes boys can be more casual about sex than girls."

Margie tried to help Sam consider what could happen. "What if you had sex, and then broke up?" she asked. "Sometimes people who've been intimate with another person feel shame and embarrassment. Once you've shared that intimacy," Margie says, "there's no going back." She wanted Sam to remember that when making his choices.

When Sam went to boarding school for the tenth grade, Margie gave him condoms. She told him, "This doesn't mean I encourage you to have sex. It just means that if you do, be safe about it. Remember what we've discussed — both the emotional and physical risks. And remember, condoms don't work if they're in your pocket."

Margie and Jay remind Sam of their values every step of the way. "With any risk-taking behavior, parents can't impress their values too often," Margie explains. "Each new situation gives kids the chance to find a reason to do what they want to do. I think it's a parent's role to say often what they feel is right or wrong. There are times I don't mind being the harping mom."

Some parents worry that giving kids condoms, while urging them to avoid sexual intercourse, gives a confusing message. Margie disagrees. Kids learn at a young age about sex from friends and the media. "They aren't getting any new ideas about sexual intercourse from us," she says.

Jay and Margie want Sam to understand that they want to protect him, no matter what choices he makes.

> *"…remember, condoms don't work if they're in your pocket."*
>
> Margie

Has it worked? Jay says it has. "Any time the subject comes up, Sam's attitude is 'Of course I know these things, Dad. Of course I would protect myself.' " And because of the relationship they've built, Jay trusts his son to tell the truth.

Consider This

Dr. Rauch: Margie and Jay recognize that, if they avoid talking about condoms, they won't be able to teach Sam to protect himself and his partner during sexual intercourse. They're taking the taboo out of condoms as a discussion topic.

Dr. Satcher: They're being realistic about the pressures children face to be sexually active. Most parents want their children to wait to have sex. But half of the adolescents in the U.S. have already had sex and are at risk for unintended pregnancy and sexually transmitted diseases. Adolescents need accurate information about contraceptive methods, including condoms, so that they can reduce those risks.

Dr. Rauch: Margie and Jay were clear with Sam: they hope he waits to have sex. By giving him condoms, they're not suggesting that they expect he'll be sexually active. They're acknowledging that he'll make his own decisions. If he does decide to have sex, they

"...half of the adolescents in the U.S. have already had sex and are at risk for unintended pregnancy and sexually transmitted diseases."

Dr. Satcher

want him to know how to protect himself and his partner.

Dr. Satcher: That's exactly right. Studies show that educating children about sexuality and about condoms does not accelerate sexual behavior. Rather than promoting sexual activity, you're saying "I care about you." That's a very important point. But an important part of an honest message is that condoms aren't perfect.

Dr. Satcher

Ask Yourself

- If my child decides to have sexual intercourse, do I want him or her to have access to condoms?

- Would I be willing to give my child condoms?

- Do I believe that encouraging my child to delay sexual intercourse, and also offering information about birth control and condoms, is a confusing message?

- Have I talked with my child about the importance of using latex condoms correctly if he or she has intercourse?

- Do I remind my child that even when using latex condoms sexual intercourse carries some degree of risk?

"Studies show that educating children about sexuality and about condoms does not accelerate sexual behavior."

Remember

Condom use has increased among ninth- through twelfth graders nationwide. Nearly 60 percent of students surveyed report that they or their partners used a condom during their last sexual intercourse.[44]

It's important that young people be reminded that latex condoms offer the best possible protection when used perfectly — consistently and correctly. (see p. 89: How to use a condom correctly)

Margie and Jay talked openly with their son Sam about condoms. As Dr. Rauch explains, in doing so they're taking the taboo out of condoms as a discussion topic. When condoms aren't considered a taboo subject, it's easier to talk with young people about what it means to use them perfectly. And it's more likely your child will learn to feel comfortable talking about condoms with a potential partner.

Judd's story

I found out we were going to have sex education in school. I didn't want to feel like a total idiot, so I started to ask my dad a lot of questions. Sex isn't a taboo subject. I can talk to him about anything. But he told me things he hadn't told me before.

My dad got a condom and said, "Here's a man's best friend." I asked what it was. A balloon? I had no idea. He said, "It's a condom. It's what you put over your penis when you have sex so you don't have a baby or get an STD." He explained that when you have sex, some diseases can be passed through you into someone else or from someone else into you. I thought: Well, I guess it is a man's best friend. And I guess it's a girl's best friend, too.

In sex ed class we learned that latex condoms are the best. Then they showed us how to use them.

I respect my dad more than anybody in the world. He shares his experiences with me. He was married when he was 20. He had my brother a year later. My brother wasn't a mistake, but my dad told me it's not easy to raise a kid and do what you want with your life.

I've never had unprotected sex. Even if a girl is on the pill, I use a condom. Except for not having sex, it's a way to be safer. We wouldn't want to have a kid or get an STD. And I

> *"You have to respect the person you're having sex with."*
>
> Judd

wouldn't want a girl to have to make a tough decision that she'd never forget. You have to respect the person you're having sex with.

Although people say sex feels better without a condom, I have the rest of my life for that. I can have unprotected sex when I'm in a monogamous relationship with someone I hope to spend the rest of my life with.

It is well documented that latex condoms, used consistently and correctly, are highly effective in preventing pregnancy and HIV. Most experts believe that latex condoms, used properly, can greatly reduce the risk of other STIs.[45] More studies are needed to measure how effectively condoms prevent STIs. The U.S. Centers for Disease Control and Prevention states that the lack of data about condom effectiveness in preventing STIs indicates more research is needed — not that latex condoms don't work.[46]

Sixty percent of young people surveyed said they used a condom the last time they had intercourse.[47] But using condoms correctly is important. Many young people have misconceptions about how to use condoms correctly.[48]

The World Health Organization (WHO) reports that the estimated pregnancy rates for couples who report using a condom correctly every time they have intercourse is three percent after one year. In couples who use condoms incorrectly or not every time they have intercourse, the pregnancy rate is 10 to 14 percent. WHO points out the higher pregnancy rate is due primarily to inconsistent and incorrect use, not condom failure. WHO states that condoms breaking or slipping off completely during intercourse is uncommon.[49]

Part of being a loving parent is seeking out and learning information that helps you talk with your child comfortably and knowledgeably.

Remember: Using a condom perfectly is using it correctly, from start to finish, every time a person has intercourse.

How to use a condom correctly

1. Choose a latex condom.

2. Store condoms carefully in a cool, dry place. Air, light, and heat can weaken latex.

3. Lubricated condoms are less likely to break. Some condoms are lubricated when you buy them. If you lubricate your own condoms, use a water-based lubricant. Petroleum or oil-based lubricants weaken latex.

4. Check the expiration date on the condom package. If the date has passed, the condom is not safe to use.

5. When opening the condom package, make sure you don't rip a hole in the condom.

6. Put the condom on an erect penis before any contact with a partner's genitals.

7. Pinch the tip of the condom to get any air out of the tip so there's room for the semen.

8. Holding on to the tip of the condom, roll it all the way onto the erect penis.

9. Have more than one condom available. If you make a mistake putting it on, for example if you put it on inside out, throw it away and use a new one.

10. After ejaculation, while the penis is still erect, hold the rim of the condom against the base of the penis and withdraw. This keeps the semen inside the condom.

11. Throw the used condom away. A condom can only be used once.

For more information about condoms, visit www.abouthealth.com.

Living with HIV

Antigone and Gail

"I had a really hard time being assertive. I rarely asked a guy to wear a condom."

Antigone

Many people think that HIV happens only to certain types of people. Parents need to remind children that HIV doesn't discriminate. It's one's behavior, not his or her background, that puts someone at risk.

It's also important to remind young people that using drugs, including alcohol, affects their ability to make good choices and increases their risk of contracting a sexually transmitted infection.

Antigone earned good grades in high school but still felt unsure of herself. Like a lot of teens, she sometimes used sex to connect with guys and to get approval. "If you felt ugly or not accepted," Antigone says, "sex was like 'Wow, someone wants me. I must be O.K.' "

Antigone was also drinking a lot. The combination of alcohol and low self-esteem made her especially vulnerable. "I had a really hard time being assertive," she says. "I rarely asked a guy to wear a condom."

Antigone didn't think about what could happen if she had sex. She and her mom Gail were close, but they'd never talked about sex or the infections you could get — infections such as herpes or HIV.

"So many parents aren't willing to accept that teenagers are sexual," Gail says. "It's partly a privacy issue. There are boundaries with your kids you sometimes don't know how to approach."

Although Gail had gay friends who had AIDS, it never occurred to her that someone who was heterosexual, much less her own child, was at risk for HIV.

Although Gail had gay friends who had AIDS, it never occurred to her that someone who was heterosexual, much less her own child, was at risk for HIV.

Gail's own drinking further complicated her relationship with her daughter. "I stopped drinking when Antigone was 16," Gail says. "But when she was growing up, I didn't set a very good example with alcohol use or in my relationships."

Antigone quit drinking when she was 20 years old. She finally felt hope when she looked to the future. "I had dreams and goals," she says. "I was really happy."

One day, a friend asked Antigone to go with him to be tested for HIV. She agreed, certain she'd be O.K. But a few days later, when it was time to get the results, she was scared and asked her mother to go with her. At the clinic, Antigone heard the devastating news. She tested positive for HIV. "Oh my God," she thought. "I'm gonna die." Overwhelmed, all she could do was to ask for her mother.

Gail and Antigone held each other and cried. "It was really horrible," Antigone says. "The look in my mom's eyes was so sad. Basically, she'd just learned her daughter was going to die."

"I felt totally hopeless and powerless," Gail says. "My first thought was I'd trade places with her, if I could."

Gail has spent many hours since that day thinking about what she might have done differently. "Oh, I have 10 million regrets," Gail says. "I wish I'd talked with Antigone about sex, but that's just the beginning."

Gail also wishes she'd raised her daughter to feel good about herself—to be confident enough to make good choices. "You can talk about abstinence all day long," she says, "but it won't matter if a child doesn't have self-esteem and uses sex to fill that void."

Antigone tested positive for HIV 13 years ago. Now, taking medications three times a day, she's doing well physically. But she's still afraid. "There's no cure," she says, "so I still

> *"The look in my mom's eyes was so sad. Basically, she'd just learned her daughter was going to die."*
>
> Antigone

worry that I'll die from this. The fear isn't as powerful as it was, but it's still there."

With help from a therapist and support from others in recovery from alcoholism, Antigone now feels emotionally strong.

"I understand myself better," she says. "I know I'm smart and good at my job. And I'm in a healthy, loving relationship. I've grown enough to know I'm more than my disease."

Antigone

Antigone wants parents to teach their children to trust and love themselves. "It's a parent's job to give children an understanding that they're O.K., that they're important to the world, to their family, and to themselves."

"When young people really believe that," Antigone says, "they're less likely to seek out-side approval through peers, drugs, or sex."

Gail agrees. She hopes parents will remind their kids that they have a right to make healthy choices. "I'd ask parents to keep work-ing on talking with kids about sex. It takes practice. But keep trying. It could save your child's life."

"... keep working on talking with kids about sex. It takes practice. But keep trying. It could save your child's life."

Gail

Consider This

Dr. Rauch: There are many lessons to learn from Antigone and Gail. The challenge for parents of teens is to be proactive so they don't have to bear heartache later on.

Dr. Satcher: When parents are reluctant to confront issues of sexuality, the consequences can be grave. And sexuality is more than having intercourse. It's about self-concept, feeling good about yourself and your potential.

Dr. Rauch: Many parents struggle to find the words or the right time to talk about sex. They often hope that their children aren't having sex. So the idea that their child is vulnerable to HIV is even more difficult for them to imagine.

Dr Satcher: Parents can prepare themselves for these conversations by talking with other adults to gain skills and information.

Dr. Rauch: And we need to go beyond teaching children how HIV is transmitted. Antigone reminds us that we need to teach children to trust and love themselves. Teens who recognize that they have talents, and who have a caring adult invested in their well-being, are much more able to meet challenges and protect themselves.

Dr. Satcher: It's important to remind our children often: "You are special. You are valued."

Teens under 15 who have ever used alcohol are twice as likely to have had sexual intercourse than their peers who have never used alcohol.[51]

Our actions show young people this. Listen to your children. Spend time with them. If we're not successful at giving children a sense of self-worth, they're vulnerable to those who will take advantage of them sexually. Children need to feel special, wanted, and nurtured.

Dr. Rauch: Gail's honesty about her own behavior is a powerful reminder that parents' actions, not just their words, influence their children.

Dr. Rauch

Ask Yourself

- Do I believe that HIV affects only certain types of people?

- Am I knowledgeable about HIV and how one can and cannot get infected with the virus?

- Antigone suggests that building children's self-esteem helps them make better choices. How do I let my child know that I think he or she is special?

- Do I remind my child that someone's behavior not background puts him or her at risk for HIV?

- How do I remind my child that alcohol affects his or her ability to make good choices?

"Parents' actions, not just their words, influence their children."

Remember

Children who feel connected to their parents and other adults they trust tend to make healthier choices. As Antigone says, when kids feel important to their families and to themselves, they're less likely to seek outside approval through peers, drugs, or sex.

Parents are the primary sexuality educators for their children. When parents avoid talking about sex, they're communicating that topics of sex and sexuality are taboo. When these discussions about sexuality do occur, they can often be negative, judgmental or punitive. Throughout a child's life, honest communication about sexual matters is essential. Parents who show each other respect and affection are positive role models throughout their children's lives. An open, honest family dialogue encourages responsible sexual behavior in children and can result in optimal sexual health.

William R. Stayton, *Th.D., Ph.D.*
Professor and Director
Human Sexuality Programs
Widener University

Veronica's story

When I found out I had HIV, my reaction was anger, shock. I didn't believe it could be happening to me. I was 19 years old, in the prime of my life.

The message I have for parents is to listen to your kids. Be open-minded with them. Let them know that they can talk to you, and that they don't have to get the information from their little friend down the street who might not know as much as she thinks she knows. Parents need to teach their children about sex and how to be safe. They don't want to be grandparents when they're 30 or lose their kids to AIDS. People die from this disease. HIV knows no race, no color, no age limits.

Home is where you get your nurturing. I remember how hard it was to talk to my parents. I was afraid they wouldn't understand. Then I learned to give my mom a chance. In the long run, I found out she knew a lot more than I gave her credit for. If only I'd listened.

"The message I have for parents is listen to your kids. Be open-minded with them."

Veronica

When your child is gay

Patrick

Feelings of confusion, fear, and rejection can lead to significantly higher use of drugs among gay youth than among heterosexual youth. Studies have reported that gay youth are up to three times more likely than their heterosexual peers to attempt suicide.[53]

When a family loves and accepts a gay child, these risks can be greatly reduced.

By the time Patrick was 11 years old, he felt that he was different.

In the sixth grade, Patrick learned what it meant to be gay. That's when he began to wonder whether the word applied to him. In school, some kids started to call him "faggot" and "homo."

Patrick remembers one of the worst days. He was teased in every class. When he raised his hand to answer a question, his classmates whispered, "Faggot, no one wants to know what you think."

Patrick was devastated. The fact that teachers overheard but ignored the comments made him feel worse. "It was so depressing," Patrick says. "My opinion didn't matter. *I* didn't matter."

He avoided the lunchroom, where the teasing continued. Kids called him a "walking disease." Sometimes he would try to get away from it all by escaping to the nurse's office.

After school, Patrick would rush home and retreat to his bedroom. He'd listen to music or play the piano. He'd cry or punch a pillow to release his anger. He felt close to his parents, but they had no clue what was happening to him at school. If they heard Patrick cry, he'd make up a story that he'd blown a test or had fought with a friend.

Patrick's mom Linda believed him. "The nurse never called," she says. "He never asked for help. Kids that age tend to spend a lot of time in their rooms. He always told us he was O.K."

By the eighth grade, Patrick was handsome and nearly six feet tall. Sometimes he'd walk down the street with his female friends. He'd see another girl and say, "She's cute. I think I'll ask her out." They'd tell him, "Patrick, you don't want to date her. You like guys." His best friends accepted what he still denied.

When Patrick finally began to believe he might be gay, he felt afraid. What if someone beat

Students who identified themselves as gay, lesbian, or bisexual were three times more likely than their peers to miss school because of feeling unsafe.[54]

him up? He'd heard plenty of stories about "gay bashing."

And what if his parents found out and got angry? What if they kicked him out of the house? "That's what every gay kid fears," Patrick says.

The summer before his freshman year, Patrick felt so afraid, he wouldn't leave the house. He played computer games, from morning till night. His mom kept saying that something was wrong. But Patrick assured her he was O.K.

Back at school in the fall, Patrick's anxiety became unbearable. Some mornings, the nurse would call for Linda to come to get him.

"He'd get into the car," Linda recalls. "His hands would be soaked with perspiration, his face white as a sheet." It was agonizing for Linda to see her son in despair. She didn't know what to do.

"I don't know what it is," Patrick said. "I can't be around people." After a few weeks, his mom insisted he see a doctor.

Patrick began to see a therapist every week. During those appointments, Patrick described the name-calling and admitted his fears. With the therapist's help, Patrick built an internal defense: he repeated to himself that he was O.K. and deserved to be treated with respect. At last, Patrick told his therapist that he was sexually attracted to guys. He was gay.

One day, Linda went with him to therapy. "I've got something to tell you, Mom," Patrick said. "I'm gay."

Linda says her heart broke. "I looked at my little boy sitting there, crying his heart out and wondering what I was thinking," Linda recalls. "I got out of my chair and knelt in front of him." I said, 'Thank you for telling me, Patrick. I love you. Whatever it takes, we'll get through this together.' " Linda and Patrick cried all the way home.

That night, Patrick refused to tell his father Peter. "I was afraid he'd hate me," Patrick says. So Linda told him instead.

Then, Peter went to Patrick's room and pulled up a chair. "Mom says you're gay," Peter said. "Listen to me. It doesn't matter. I love you. I want to be a part of your life."

Patrick and his dad hugged and cried. "It was huge to get that off my shoulders," Patrick says. "My brothers and sisters have been great, too. They've all totally accepted me."

At school, Patrick slowly started to defend himself. Kids would call him "faggot," and he'd ask, "Why would you say that? So what if I am?" The bullies began to leave him alone. The more Patrick stood up for himself, the less fearful he felt.

"Thank you for telling me, Patrick. I love you. Whatever it takes, we'll get through this together."

Linda

Patrick feels like the luckiest guy alive. "If I'd known my parents would accept me the way they did," he says, "I'd have told them years earlier. It would have saved me so much self-hate."

Looking back, Linda says there were moments when she had suspected that her son was gay, but she blocked it out. She still feels sad and guilty that he suffered so long in silence.

"If I'd known my parents would accept me the way they did, I'd have told them years earlier."

Patrick

"Parents dream of their kids getting married and having kids," she says. "I didn't want to let that go. But thank God Patrick trusted me. Thank God he told me."

Not long after telling his parents he was gay, Patrick had the lead role in a school play, "Pippin." Patrick told his mom and dad to listen carefully to one particular song. "I'll be singing about myself," he said. "And most of the audience won't even know it."

On stage Patrick sang: "Why do I feel I don't fit in anywhere I go? I've got to be where my spirit runs free. I have to find my corner of the sky." As they listened, Linda and Peter cried tears of joy knowing that Patrick finally understood and accepted himself.

They still worry every day about Patrick's safety. But Peter and Linda believe that he's finally at peace with himself. "It makes me so happy," Linda says. "He's excited to go to school now.

His friendships are strong. He's being asked to act in regional theaters."

Linda and Peter hope other people can learn from their experience. "We have an obligation to understand and support our children, no matter what," Linda says. "You don't cast them away. They aren't disposable. Patrick didn't ask to be born. How can we ask him to be someone other than who he is?"

"If parents can't accept that their child is gay, I would suggest they consider this: Why are they worried about what other people think?" Peter says. "It's *their* child."

Studies report that gay children are more likely to attempt suicide. Knowing Patrick's anguish, Linda and Peter understand why.

"What I'd say to other parents is this," Linda says. " 'Make a choice. Love them or bury them.' We chose to love."

"What I'd say to other parents is this: 'Make a choice. Love them or bury them.' We chose to love."

Linda

Consider This

Dr. Rauch: You couldn't ask for a better example of a parent's unconditional love. Not every parent will respond so well. Sometimes parents wish they had responded differently when they learned that their child was gay. They can go back to their child and say, "I was surprised by what you shared. My reaction may have hurt your feelings or made you think that I don't love you."

Dr. Satcher

"Patrick's parents gave him the most important message: We love you. We respect you. And we're always going to be here for you."

Dr. Satcher: We live in a society where many people have difficulty dealing with homosexuality. These parents are to be commended for how well they handled the situation. Both of Patrick's parents gave him the most important message: "We love you. We respect you. And we're always going to be here for you."

Dr. Rauch: It's easy for children to imagine that the people who love them most won't love them if they're gay. That's why they often keep it a secret. Even though Linda didn't know why Patrick was struggling, she sought professional help. Many parents who suspect their child may be gay don't know how to bring up the issue. Some worry that asking questions will influence their child's sexuality. That's not true. Asking questions and talking about homosexuality won't make children gay.

Dr. Satcher: It's sad when children feel they're not able to talk about their sexual orientation. I'm sure that Patrick wishes he'd talked with his parents earlier. But it's difficult for young people to feel safe doing so. There's evidence that this fear probably contributes to self-destructive behavior, including suicide, among gay youth.

Dr. Rauch: In any classroom of 25 or 30 students it's likely there's more than one gay child. It's painful to know that some educators fail to intervene when children bully others with homophobic slurs. Sometimes teachers who wouldn't ever allow ethnic slurs in the classroom will ignore homophobic slurs. We all share in the responsibility of making sure educators recognize that ignoring harassment can have serious long-term consequences for the child.

Dr. Satcher: School boards, boards of education, and parent and teacher organizations need to take a role in training all school personnel to a create safe and productive learning environments for all children.

Dr. Rauch: It was heartbreaking for Linda to see that Patrick was so worried about how she'd respond. Some parents may be so overwhelmed by learning that their child is gay that they're unable to be supportive. It's important that parents who are struggling find individual or group support to handle their own emotions. This will help them be a supportive force in their child's life.

Dr. Satcher: The primary message to a child who is gay needs to include reassurance. Homosexuality may not always be easy for children but they can count on their parents' love.

Dr. Rauch

"In any classroom of 25 or 30 students it's likely there's more than one gay child."

Ask Yourself

- How do I encourage my child to be respectful of all people?

- If my child told me he or she were gay, how would I want to respond?

- How do I show my child unconditional love?

- How do I let my child know it's safe to talk with me about sexual feelings, regardless of his or her sexual orientation?

- If I realized that my child was struggling emotionally, would I seek professional help for him or her?

- What policies does my child's school have against bullying and harassment?

"Definitely let your kid know it's O.K. if they are gay."

Patrick

Remember

Many gay adults say that as adolescents they felt different, but didn't understand why. As a parent, you can't predict whether your child will be gay. It's important to create an environment where your child feels unconditionally loved. A child who feels accepted is more likely to bring his or her concerns to you.

Patrick's story

Before I told my parents I was gay, the fear they wouldn't accept me was overwhelming. Now, knowing that my parents are there for me is incredible. It makes everything better.

I see so many stories on the news, and hear from other kids who are gay, that their families don't accept them. My parents totally trust me. I know they support me.

Parents need to know that a child they love may be gay. Unless your child tells you, you won't know. Definitely let your kid know it's O.K. if they are gay.

There are ways to bring up the subject. For example, when parents see things about the gay community on TV, they need to be aware of comments they make. If they are support-ive, children who are gay will feel they can trust their parents to accept them.

There are probably hard times ahead for me. I am fully prepared for discrimination. There are people who are against homosexuals. I've dealt with them before, and I'll probably have to deal with them again. But the love from my parents helps me cope with cruel comments. I know my parents love me. It makes me love myself more.

Creating an environment of love and acceptance in your home.

As a parent, it's important to let your child know that he or she is loved and accepted, regardless of sexual orientation. One way to begin a conversation is to ask your child about his or her developing sexuality. "How do you feel about dating?" "Is there someone you are attracted to?" "What do you like about that person?"

These kinds of questions tell children that you're interested in them. Children who are struggling with their sexual orientation often won't bring up concerns the first time you talk with them about relationships. Watch for opportunities to follow up.

For example, your child mentions he is going to a party. You can ask, "Are any of your friends going out with someone?" "Are any in a same-sex relationship?" He may respond by saying none of his friends are gay. You can say that may appear to be the case, because it takes courage to admit to being gay. Especially in a world that sometimes rejects homosexuals. You can tell him he may find out later that some of his friends are in fact gay.

Dr. Rauch

Endnotes

1. *Adolescent Development and the Biology of Puberty,* workshop summary on new research, National Research Council Institute of Medicine; Board on Children, Youth, and Families, National Academy of Sciences, National Academy Press, 1999, p. 1.

2. Adapted from Mayes LC, Cohen DJ, *The Yale Child Development Study Center Guide to Understanding Your Child,* Little Brown, 2002, p. 196.

3. Ibid. p. 196.

4. National Research Council, et. al., p. 1.

5. *With One Voice: America's Adults and Teens Sound Off About Teen Pregnancy,* National Survey, National Campaign To Prevent Teen Pregnancy, December 2003.

6. "Virginity and The First Time," SexSmarts Survey, Kaiser Family Foundation/*Seventeen Magazine,* October 2003.

7. Dittus PJ, Jaccard J, "Adolescents' Perceptions of Maternal Disapproval of Sex: Relationship to Sexual Outcomes," *Journal of Adolescent Health,* 2000, Vol. 26, pp. 268-78.

8. Kaiser Family Foundation/*Seventeen Magazine,* October 2003.

9. "Communication," SexSmarts Survey, Kaiser Family Foundation/*Seventeen Magazine,* July 2002.

10. National Research Council, et. al., p. 8.

11. Adapted from Pamela Zuckerman, M.D., *Raising Healthy Kids: Families Talk About Sexual Health,* Family Health Productions, Inc. 2000.

12. *Talking with Kids About Tough Issues,* Kaiser Family Foundation/Children Now National Surveys: Menlo Park, CA, Kaiser Family Foundation, 1997.

13. Adapted from Mayes LC, Cohen DJ, *The Yale Child Development Study Center Guide to Understanding Your Child,* pp. 399-400.

14. Kaiser Family Foundation, 1997.

15. The Alan Guttmacher Institute, unpublished tabulations of 1995 National Survey of Adolescent Men and 1995 National Survey of Family Growth.

16. Cohen DA, Farley TA, Taylor SN, Martin DH, Schuster MA, "When and Where Do Youths Have Sex? The Potential Role of Adult Supervision," *Pediatrics,* Vol. 110, No. 6, December 2002, p. e66.

17. *Teens Talk About Dating, Intimacy and Their Sexual Experiences,* Kaiser Family Foundation National Survey of Teens: Menlo Park, CA, Kaiser Family Foundation, 1998.

18. National Campaign to Prevent Teen Pregnancy, December 2003.

19. Kaiser Family Foundation, 1997.

20. King K, Holmes KK, Sparling PF, Per-Anders M, Lemon SM, Stamm W, *Sexually Transmitted Diseases,* 3rd ed., McGraw-Hill, New York, 1999.

21. Hitchcock PJ, MacKay T, Wasserheit JN, Binder R (eds.), *STDs and Adverse Outcomes of Pregnancy,* ASM Press, Washington, DC, 1999.

22. *Workshop Summary: Scientific Evidence on Condom Effectiveness for Sexually Transmitted Disease (STD) Prevention,*

National Institute of Allergy and Infectious Diseases, National Institutes of Health, Department of Health and Human Services, June 12-13, 2000, Herndon, Virginia.

[23] Ashley R, *Sexually Transmitted Diseases,* Lippincott, Williams & Wikins, Vol. 29, No. 10, October 2002.

[24] Corey L, Wald A, Patel R, Sacks SL, Tyring SK, Warren T, Douglas JM, Paavonen J, Ashley R, Beutner KR, Stratchounsky LS, Mertz G, Keene ON, Watson HA, Tait D, Vargas-Cortes M, for the Valacyclovir HSV Transmission Study Group, "Once-Daily Valacyclovir to Reduce the Risk of Transmission of Genital Herpes," *New England Journal of Medicine,* January 1, 2004, Vol. 350(1), pp. 67-8.

[25] Brown ZA, Wald A, Ashley R, Selke S, Zeh J, Corey L, "Effect of Serologic Status and Cesarean Delivery on Transmission Rates of Herpes Simplex Virus From Mother to Infant," *Journal of the American Medical Association,* January 2003, Vol. 289, pp. 203-209.

[26] Burk RD, "Human Papillomavirus and the Risk of Cervical Cancer," *Hospital Practice,* November 15, 1999.

[27] Palefsky JM, Holly EA, Hogeboom CJ, Jay N, Berry MJ, Darragh TM, "Anal Cytology as a Screening Tool for Anal Squamous Intraepithelial Lesions," *Journal of Acquired Immune Deficiency Syndromes & Human Retrovirology,* Vol. 14(5), pp. 415-422, April 15, 1997.

[28] Abma JC, Sonenstein FL, *Sexual Activity and Contraceptive Practices Among Teenagers in the United States, 1988 and 1995,* National Center for Health Statistics, Vital Health Stat 23(21), 2001.

[29] Miller KS, Levin ML, Whitaker DJ, Xu X, "Patterns of Condom Use Among Adolescents: The impact of maternal-adolescent communication," *American Journal of Public Health,* Vol. 88, pp. 1542-1544, 1998.

[30] The Alan Guttmacher Institute (AGI), Teenage pregnancy: overall trends and state-by-state information, New York: AGI, 1999, Table 1; and Henshaw SK, U.S. Teenage pregnancy statistics with comparative statistics for women aged 20-24, New York: AGI, 1999, p. 5.

[31] The Alan Guttmacher Institute, *Sex and America's Teenagers,* New York: AGI, 1994, p. 38.

[32] Weinstock H, Berman S, Cates W, "Sexually Transmitted Diseases Among American Youth: Incidence and Prevalence Estimates, 2000," *Perspectives in Sexual and Reproductive Health,* US Centers for Disease Control and Prevention, January/February 2004.

[33] Piccinino LJ, Mosher WD, "Trends in Contraceptive Use in the United States: 1982-1995," *Family Planning Perspectives,* Vol. 30, No. 1, pp. 4-10 & 46, 1998.

[34] *Kids Count Special Report: When Teens Have Sex: Issues and Trends,* Annie E. Casey Foundation, Baltimore, MD, 1998.

[35] Hatcher RA, Trussell J, Stewart F, Cates W, Nelson A, Guest F, Kowal D, *Contraceptive Technology,* 18th Edition, New York, Arcent Media, 2004.

[36] Hatcher RA, Zieman M, Cwiak C, Darney PD, Creinin MD, Stosur HR, *Managing Contraception 2004-2005,* Bridging the Gap Communications, Inc., 2004.

[37] Adapted from Trussel J, Kowal D, "The Essentials of Contraception" in Hatcher RA et. al., *Contraceptive Technology;* 18th Edition, New York, Arcent Media, 2004.

[38] National Institutes of Health, June 2000.

[39] *Sex Education in America: A View From Inside the Nation's Classrooms,* National Public Radio/Kaiser Family Foundation/Harvard University's Kennedy School of Government Poll, January 2004.

[40] Adapted from Trussel J, Kowal D, *Contraceptive Technology,* 2004.

[41] National Institutes of Health, June 2000.

[42] Miller KS, Levin ML, Whitaker DJ, Xu X, *American Journal of Public Health,* Vol. 88, pp. 1542-1544, 1998.

[43] *National Survey of Adolescents and Young Adults: Sexual Health Knowledge, Attitudes and Experiences,* Menlo Park, CA, Kaiser Family Foundation, 2003.

[44] *Youth Risk Behavior Surveillance — United States, 2001,* Morbidity and Mortality Weekly Report, Vol. 51, (SS04), pp. 1-64, US Centers for Disease Control and Prevention, June 28, 2002.

[45] *Condoms and Sexually Transmitted Diseases... especially AIDS,* U.S. Food and Drug Administration, September 2003.

[46] *Latex Condoms and Sexually Transmitted Diseases – Prevention Messages,* U.S. Centers for Disease Control and Prevention, Atlanta, GA: CDC, 2001, p.2.

[47] U.S. Centers for Disease Control and Prevention, June 28, 2002.

[48] Rosenberg J, "Young People in the United States are Often Misinformed About the Proper Use of Condoms", *Family Planning Perspectives,* Vol. 33, No. 5, p. 235, September/October 2001.

[49] World Health Organization, Fact Sheet #243, June 2000.

[50] Kaiser Family Foundation, 1997.

[51] *Dangerous Liaisons: Substance Abuse and Sex,* The National Center on Addiction and Substance Abuse, Columbia University, 1999.

[52] *Making Schools Safe for Gay and Lesbian Youth: Report of the Massachusetts Governor's Commission on Gay and Lesbian Youth,* 1993.

[53] Garofalo R, Wolf RC, Kessel S, Palfrey J, DuRant RH, "The Association Between Health Risk Behaviors and Sexual Orientation Among a School-based Sample of Adolescents," *Pediatrics,* Vol.101, No.5, May 1998.

[54] Massachusetts High School Students and Sexual Orientation Results, Massachusetts Risk Behavior Survey (MYRBS), 1999.

Acknowledgements

The parents and young people who tell their stories in this book show courage and a desire to help others learn from their experiences.

Dr. Rauch, Dr. Satcher, Dr. Hitchcock and Dr. Hatcher generously offered their knowledge, insight, and experience. In doing so they support parents in their efforts to raise children who are sexually healthy and who make good choices.

My gratitude also to Chris Thrasher, M.A., Morehouse School of Medicine; Thomas Consolati, M.ED., public school superintendent; Patricia Daoust, R.N., M.S.N.; Annie Fielding, writer; Matt James, Kaiser Family Foundation; John Hogan, adjunct professor, Northeastern University; Mark Kaplan M.D., Harvard Medical School; Larry Kessler, founder AIDS Action Committee of Massachusetts; Chad Martin, M.P.H., youth behavior specialist; Kim Miller, Ph.D., family communication researcher; Riana Riggs, photographer: Alex's photo; Dierdre Savage, content and design consultant; and Kettie MacLean, researcher.

To order *Words Can Work* books and for online columns, visit www.wordscanwork.com.

Also available:

Raising Healthy Kids: Families Talk About Sexual Health (video/DVD)

Interviews with experts, parents, and young people offer information and skills for talking with young children, preadolescents, and adolescents about sexual health. Includes discussion guides. For parents and other caregivers. Produced by Family Health Productions.

Contact:

Blake Works, Inc.
Telephone: 978.282.1663
E-mail: info@wordscanwork.com